GOD, MT. FUJI, AND SWEET TEA

ENDORSEMENTS

What a beautiful display of perseverance amid seemingly inevitable decay. *God, Mt. Fuji, and Sweet Tea* is a carefully worked piece of literature where Janet Smith lays bare and transparent the hopes and dreams of a marriage gone wrong, yet not beyond hope. Through her faith, consistent prayers, and the grace of God, the covenant she entered decades before is restored and made whole. An excellent read for those feeling stuck in a relationship that cannot be repaired.

—**Tiffany Sneed**, Col., United States Army, Marriage Ministry Leader, South Hairston A.M.E. Church.

When problems and conflict plague a marriage, the path to reigniting the love and getting past the hurt may feel too difficult to pursue. At such times, hearing the story of someone who worked through it and got to the other side can encourage us to go the distance. In *God, Mt. Fuji, and Sweet Tea*, author Janet Smith begins her memoir as a disillusioned and weary wife struggling to hold onto her marriage. Against a colorful backdrop painted for the reader through beautifully descriptive passages, Janet transports her readers into her life story to discover the transformational principles that saved her marriage. It's a story of marital redemption that can encourage others to stay the course and not give up.

—**Linda W. Rooks**, *Fighting for Your Marriage while Separated* and *Broken Heart on Hold, Surviving Separation*

This is a great story! As I read *God, Mt. Fuji, and Sweet Tea*, I felt as though Janet was having a conversation with me. The details are vivid as Janet masterfully paints a picture for readers. This story is relatable and relevant to those who are struggling in their marriages. Many women will find hope and courage as they discover Janet's story.

—**Debra Thomas**, Ed.D. Christian Education Leadership

God, Mt. Fuji, and Sweet Tea is not a how-to book on saving your marriage. It's a story about a real wife and mother who wants to save her marriage. Janet opens her heart in *God, Mt. Fuji, and Sweet Tea* and takes you on a journey from rural Georgia to the hustle and bustle of the beautiful country of Japan. There she discovers God's design for marriage, which sets her on the pathway to restoring her broken marriage. Janet's most heartbreaking moments will speak to every wife and mother who truly wants to keep her family together.

—**Christina Campbell**, adoption attorney, The Campbell Law Practice, LLC

Often women feel alone in their struggle to stay in an unhappy marriage and seek divorce as a solution. In *God, Mt. Fuji, and Sweet Tea*, Janet conveys to the reader, with prayer, a wife can find love and intimacy in her marriage again. Her prayers are woven throughout her journey as she encounters hardships and setbacks trying to reconcile with her husband. Not only is Janet transformed by her prayers, but her husband is transformed too. Whether you have given up on your marriage or want a closer relationship with your spouse, *God, Mt. Fuji, and Sweet Tea* will encourage you to get started.

—**Maxine Peaks**, Director of Women's Ministry and Christian Education, Second Baptist Church.

Janet's heart for God, her desire for a God-honoring marriage, and her passion for the man she promised to love and cherish for a lifetime flows throughout *God, Mt. Fuji, and Sweet Tea*. Janet's story is every woman's story who's ever considered giving up on her marriage. Desperate to hold onto her marriage, she journeyed with her family across the world to teach military kids and start afresh. But it was Janet who learned more than she ever dreamed possible—about herself, her marriage, and a faithful God, when she climbed to the summit of Mt. Fuji. Journey with Janet through her story and you might share a similar pilgrimage to a renewed marriage and deeper relationship with the Lord.

—**Julie Lavender**, author of *365 Ways to Love Your Child: Turning Little Moments into Lasting Memories*, Revell/Baker Publishing Group

GOD, MT. FUJI, AND SWEET TEA

Janet Paige Smith

ELK LAKE PUBLISHING INC

PUBLISHING THE POSITIVE
Plymouth, Massachusetts

Cover and Interior Design: Tamara Dever, Derinda Babcock

Editor(s): Peggy Ellis, Deb Haggerty

Author Represented By: Credo Communications LLC

PUBLISHED BY: Elk Lake Publishing, Inc., 35 Dogwood Drive, Plymouth, MA 02360, 2020

Library Cataloging Data

Names: Smith, Janet Paige

God, Mt. Fuji, and Sweet Tea / Janet Paige Smith

194 p. 23cm × 15cm (9in × 6 in.)

Identifiers: ISBN-13: 978-1-64949-186-2 (paperback) | 978-1-64949-187-9 (trade paperback) | 978-1-64949-188-6 (e-book)

Key Words: marriage; relationships; family; love & marriage; spiritual growth & renewal; women's interests; inspirational

LCCN: 2021938841 Nonfiction

DEDICATION

David, Ryyan, and Laughlin, I've watched you overcome challenging situations, stand up for what you believe in, and seek Godly wisdom. I'm proud to be your mom.

Mark, thank you for supporting me throughout the years in my desire to become a writer and allowing me to share our story.

Curtis and Johnnie Marie Paige, thank you for showing me how to love God and family and never give up.

CONTENTS

ACKNOWLEDGMENTS

To the Department of Defense School System (DODDS) for considering us for employment. You recognized our qualifications and gave us the privilege of joining an elite group of teachers who educate service members' children living in foreign countries. Thank you for the tremendous role you play in providing a quality education for children of the men and women who serve our country.

To Hattie Phipps, a gift to all God's children, a special thanks for hiring us both, taking us into your team of teachers, and treating us like family.

To the students we taught and their parents at Shirley Lanham Elementary School for challenging us to be academically, physically, and emotionally ready to teach each day. Thank you for the privilege to teach you.

To Debra Thomas, whose prayers and many calls throughout the years asking about my book kept me working. Without your gentle prodding, the book would still be on my pin drive. You are the best!

Christina Campbell, Julie Lavender, Maxine Peaks, Linda W. Rooks, Col. Tiffany Sneed, and Dr. Debra Thomas who took time from your super busy schedules to read my manuscript and write a great endorsement for my book. I will always remember your kindness and generosity.

My Guideposts family, who selected me as a Guideposts Workshop winner and taught me how to write inspirationally. I appreciate the opportunity you've given me to share my articles about God's love for families and the confidence to write a book.

Susan K. Stewart, who joined me at a table with a group of writers and listened to my story during the Mt. Hermon Christian Writers Conference. Years later, after becoming the Managing Editor–Nonfiction for Elk Lake, you remembered me and asked for the book. Thank you for your confidence in my ability to write a compelling story.

Deb Haggerty and Tim Beals, for taking a chance on a first-time book author and believing readers would be encouraged by my story. You are both professionals in your field and also mentors to new writers. Thank you for picking up the phone or quickly emailing me and patiently answering my questions.

My editors, Peggy Ellis and Tracy Donley, thank you for asking the tough questions and making me dig deeper into my story. You both made my words sound great.

Tamara Dever, for listening to God's voice and designing a beautiful book cover for *God, Mt. Fuji, and Sweet Tea.*

A big thank you to Mamie Williams and her walking partners, my first beta readers, who gave me loving feedback and encouragement to continue writing.

All of Mark's and my stateside school teachers, family members, friends, and church members who encouraged me to keep writing. Your kinds words were needed and appreciated.

David, Ryyan, Laughlin and my new daughter-in-law, Avery—you all pushed me to think, act, and invest in myself as a professional writer. Thank you for not giving up on me.

Most importantly, a loving thank you to my husband, Mark, who allowed me to share our story.

Thank you, God, for sending me on a journey and helping me write the story.

CHAPTER 1—THE INTERVIEW

"If we don't get hired before the summer, I'm not going anywhere," Mark said, grabbing his hat and marching down the porch steps into Georgia's sweltering heat. I slumped onto the rocking chair. We'd waited months for an interview, and with summer break in a week, my hopes of teaching overseas faded.

Tears spilled over, blurring the tin-topped barn nestled along the hay field where our boys played. After years of marriage, our sons are what held us together, like twine around bales of hay.

My marriage was in trouble, and Mark refused to admit anything was wrong. No date nights or counseling had solved our problems. Divorce was my way out.

A ping from incoming email drew me into the house. The subject line read: Possible Employment Opportunities. I clicked open the email. I would like to conduct interviews with you by phone on Saturday, 31 May at 1 p.m. EDT. Thanks for your interest in the Department of Defense School System. Ms. Phipps.

May thirty-first was today. My heart pounding, I printed the message and hurried outside. I shielded my eyes from the blazing sun, waving the email as Mark's tractor rumbled from the garden toward me.

"Why are you so excited?" Mark said, shutting off the 8N tractor and jumping to the ground.

"Read this," I said, my hand shaking.

"You've been waiting for this," he said, wiping sweat from his brow.

"Eleven o'clock," he said, glancing at his watch. "We have two hours before the interview."

I smiled rereading the email, then doubt crept in. How are we going to answer questions together during an interview when we can't have a conversation without arguing?

Where was Mark? I glanced out the kitchen window. In the garden, yellow squash petals drooped under the hot sun. I'd reminded him an hour ago about the interview. Studying my notes, I paced the kitchen floor.

Mark strolled through the kitchen door, carrying a basket of vegetables, dropping dirt clods from the garden, his jeans and white T-shirt streaked with soil.

"Do you have to cook now?"

"Relax," he said, washing vegetables in the sink. "I can answer questions and cook too."

The phone rang. I picked up the receiver and with the speaker on, and fresh, sweet boiling corn in the air, Mark and I introduced ourselves. Ms. Phipps began the interview asking questions about our philosophies on education and assessing student achievement. Mark answered with ease while removing corn from a steaming pot. I fumbled through my notes stuttering my answers.

Finally, the interview was over. Ms. Phipps said she needed experienced teachers like us, but she had more candidates to interview. She'd contact us in a week.

"We can't wait a week," I blurted. "We have cows to sell, hay fields to lease, and a house to pack up." I flinched in disbelief as the words flew from my mouth. Not only had I told Ms. Phipps what I couldn't do, I'd also sounded desperate. After months waiting for this interview, I'd blown it.

A nerve-wracking pause traveled the phone line.

"Okay," Ms. Phipps said, "you're both hired. Your sponsor will contact you over the summer."

Sinking into a chair, I said a quick thank you. Mark mumbled his thanks through a mouth filled with corn. I quickly hung up the phone before Ms. Phipps changed her mind. A week later, a FedEx package arrived with our contracts. We were committed for two years to teach at Shirley Lanham Elementary School and expected to arrive at the Naval Air Facility in Atsugi, Japan, by the end of summer.

The job offers were bittersweet. David, our nineteen-year-old, had deployed to Iraq a month before. He said he'd contact me when he could.

Later that day, I pulled our SUV into the military prep school parking lot where Ryyan attended school. He stood laughing and tossing a football among a group of cadets.

Spotting me, he strolled toward the SUV, his long, black tie hanging loose over his white uniform shirt. He tossed his football gear and book bag onto the backseat and slid into the passenger side.

"Dad and I have accepted teaching positions in Japan," I said, driving away from the school.

"I'll start high school in Japan?"

"Yep."

"Dad agreed to leave the farm?"

"Well, he's going," I said, checking to see his reaction. I needed Ryyan's support. He and Mark were close. Persuading Mark to go had been difficult, but trying to convince them both—impossible.

"Uh-oh. I'm going to miss playing high school football."

"You can play football in Japan."

"Mom, the Japanese don't play football," he said in his Mom-you-don't-know-anything-about-football voice.

"I mean with the American high school team."

"What about Sonny Boy? Can he come too?"

Sonny Boy, a brindle-colored mutt who chased deer through the gardens, joined our family as a puppy three years ago.

"I don't see why not."

"We'll come back in time for me to graduate with my classmates, right?"

"Sure," I stammered. My heart swelled, remembering my own high school years, interrupted by my dad's military duty assignments. The missed dances. The missed field trips. Never having a close girlfriend to giggle with over the cute boys in our class or compare hopes and dreams with. I didn't even have a yearbook to help me remember.

Smiling hard to fight back tears, I pulled into our gravel driveway.

Mom, who lived three hours away, picked up Laughlin and gladly offered to keep him over the summer. Laughlin, our surprise baby, was born a week after we buried my oldest brother. His unexpected death left a hole in my parents' hearts that only a newborn baby could fill.

We were all proud of our new addition, but having a baby in the house after nine years required everyone pitch in. David and Ryyan had to babysit and learn to change diapers.

When Laughlin became a toddler, he quickly learned playing video games is what big boys do. Soon, the boys' complaints about Laughlin's constant interruptions, and a wailing baby feeling left out, filled our home.

One day, the absence of noise in the house lured me to the family room. There, Laughlin sat on David's lap babbling and cooing at the TV screen, his chubby fingers on David's hand. Ryyan, David, and the baby were all playing a video game.

"How'd you teach him to play?" I said.

"Mom, he just thinks he's playing," they both sang out.

I walked away smiling. It wouldn't be long before Laughlin figured out their trick, but for now, we all had peace.

With Laughlin at Mom's, getting ready for our move to Japan was easier. Throughout the summer, Mark repaired the barns, sold cows, and harvested vegetables. Although Mark celebrated with me when we got the jobs, whenever I talked about Japan, he'd find reasons not to leave.

One afternoon, packing, I discovered our wedding album I'd tossed in the hall closet after an argument. My eyes moistened, looking at my twenty-one-year-old self at the altar. Mom's pearls hung around my neck, and the gown trimmed in lace she and I had picked out fit perfectly. Gazing into each other's eyes, Mark and I repeated our vows and lit a white, taper candle symbolizing our commitment to love each other forever.

Now, disillusioned with marriage, I was moving six thousand miles away to keep my promise. I caressed the wedding photo and placed the album in the box marked for Japan.

CHAPTER 2—YELLOW RIBBONS

In midsummer, a welcome packet arrived from Tony, our sponsor at Lanham Elementary School. Reading the information from the housing office on Atsugi Navy Base, my heart sank—most Japanese landlords didn't allow pets in their rental houses. How was I going to tell the boys we couldn't take Sonny Boy?

Mom and I spoke throughout the summer over the phone. I didn't discuss the trouble in my marriage. It would only worry her and Pops. She never pried, although she sensed the tension between Mark and me. "Pray about your marriage and God will make everything all right," she'd say. An Army wife, who'd moved with four children across the country, she understood the challenges I faced. Although leaving would mean an end to our weekly phone calls and visits, Mom understood moving to Japan was best for the family.

Mom and I talked about David. Neither one of us had heard from him since he'd left for Iraq. I wanted him home with us, excited about moving to Japan.

At 2:00 a.m., the caller ID flashed an out-of-country code.

"Hi, Mom. I'm in a phone booth and only have a few minutes to talk."

"David? Are you okay?" I said, quickly sitting up in the bed.

"I miss home," he said.

"I know," I said, tears forming. " Everyone's praying the war will end soon. Where are you in Iraq?"

"I can't tell you—the phones are monitored—but I'm not at the airport."

The news reported the airport as the safest place in Iraq. I couldn't let David know I was afraid for him. I changed the subject.

"We leave for Japan the end of August."

"I'm happy for you. The move will make things better between you and Dad."

Soldiers yelled in the background.

"David?"

I strained to hear his voice.

"I'm here!" David said.

"Let me get Dad. He's asleep downstairs."

"I don't have time. Gotta go. I love you, Mom." Click. The line hummed.

"I love you," I whispered.

Choking back sobs, I clutched the receiver, hoping David would somehow return. I hung up. Why couldn't it be me and not David fighting in the war? Soldiers wearing heavy vests and helmets, shooting rifles, running through the streets of Bagdad flashed through my mind. Was leaving, with David in a warzone, the right thing to do? Touching the empty space on Mark's side of the bed, I cried.

A week later, canning jars rattled as I carried them to the barn for storage. Inside, Mark swung a huge wrench at a tractor grill.

"You know taking the boys from their home is selfish, and David needs us in Georgia, not some foreign country," he said, eyes hard, dropping the wrench to the ground. I quickly placed the canning jars on a wooden shelf before the fight started.

"We've signed the contracts, and the moving company will be here tomorrow," I said, taking a deep breath and holding back my anger that if unleashed would have us yelling at each other.

"I don't care. You can cancel a contract and tell the packers not to come." His eyes softened. "If we try harder, we can make our marriage work."

"You mean like the counseling sessions you stopped going to because you said they weren't working."

"That's not fair. The guy didn't even know us, and you weren't being truthful."

"All we do is argue, and we don't even touch each other anymore," I said.

Mark walked toward me and stopped.

"How can I touch you if you're mad all the time?" he said, with pleading eyes.

Hadn't he listened to me at all? Mark, no longer the adventurous, supportive man I married, only cared about work and the farm. When we took a vacation, we visited my parents.

I stormed out the barn. Feeling sorry for Mark, giving in to him and staying would only hurt me. We'd just fall back into the cycle of arguing and then stony silence.

When I left the military, and we move to the farm where Mark grew up, I was charmed by country living. Now, I dreaded the daily monotony and isolation. His refusal to accept my unhappiness made things worse. Our fighting was robbing our children of their childhood.

Previously, after an argument, we both agreed to get away. Leaving the boys with Mom, we took a mini vacation to Washington, DC, where Mark's brother lived. Since we both like museums, his brother suggested we visit the one in the Pentagon.

At the entrance of a long corridor, a trifold sat on a table. Displayed in the middle was a large world map, and above it the words, Department of Defense School System: Travel to Exciting Places Teaching Military Children Overseas. I picked up a brochure. Inside, teachers were taking pictures with students on field trips all over the world. Hope rose up in me as I envisioned us teaching overseas.

Later that evening, I shared the brochure with Mark. He scoffed at the idea and said moving our family to a foreign country to teach was ridiculous. My high spirits plummeted along with the progress we'd made towards reconciliation during our week in DC. When we returned home, I pleaded with him again to fill out the applications, since we probably wouldn't get hired anyway. He gave in.

From the barn, clanging pierced the night air as I stomped back to the house. We'd waited months for our interview. I was leaving with or without him. We'd never get this opportunity again.

With less than a week left before our departure, we hadn't found anyone to oversee our farm. From the kitchen window, I watched Sam and Mark heave a huge, round, wicker basket loaded with the last harvested vegetables onto Sam's truck. They shook hands, and Sam drove off. Sam and his wife, Mary, were an older couple whose farm adjourned ours. Sam helped Mark with the harvest, and Mary always came to my rescue when I needed help with the boys.

Mark appeared at the kitchen door. "Sam's offered to watch the farm and has an extra pen for Sonny Boy," he said, staring past me like I was invisible—then walked away.

I felt like a two-headed monster—one head relieved because Sam would watch over the farm, and the other, full of shame because I wanted to leave my home.

The day before leaving, I returned from a last-minute shopping trip and found Mom's minivan parked in the driveway. Laughlin's suitcase lay on the kitchen floor, and Mom stood at the stove turning sizzling meat in a frying pan. Flour spattered the countertop, and a pound cake pan brimming with batter sat by the oven.

"Mom, we catch a plane in the morning. Do you know how long it took me to pack up the kitchen?" I said, ready to allow the stress of moving to burst forth like an unclogged kitchen sink.

"I'll clean it up," she snapped, poking a fork hard into the meat. "My grandchildren need a decent meal before they leave."

"You're right," Mom," I said hugging her. "Who knows when we'll get another opportunity to eat a home-cooked meal." Her watery eyes reflected sadness. Mom's life revolved around her grandchildren. She drove three hours to attend their school and sporting events, spent time with them during the summer, and never missed a birthday. Dabbing at our tears and smiling, we placed food on the table and chuckled, remembering the many celebration meals we'd cooked together.

Mom, the boys, and I stayed up late having fun together. With a few weeks of summer left, warm air and noise from chirping crickets and croaking frogs pushed inside the house, while I went from room to room packing suitcases. Mom cradled Laughlin in her arms as she read a picture book about Japan to him. When he fell asleep, she went into Ryyan's room and sat on his bed. His chin cupped in both hands, he smiled while she lectured him on helping around the house, keeping up his grades, and being a big brother.

After breakfast the next morning, she and I cleaned the countertops and stored the dishes in plastic containers under the cabinet.

The kitchen was spotless when Mom pulled out the driveway headed home.

"I can't believe we're leaving our home," Mark said on the morning of our departure. He stared out our bedroom window at the plowed-up gardens and vacant hay fields where the cows use to graze. I touched his shoulder to comfort him. He cringed. Fighting back tears, I packed the last suitcase, and braced myself for the argument ready to roll in like a summer storm. Instead, Mark closed our suitcases and carried them downstairs.

I picked up my carry-on bag and turned to the door, casting one last glance at the bride and groom figurine I'd salvaged from our wedding. Wiping tears, I took a deep breath and hurried downstairs.

Mark drove the rental van slowly down our gravel driveway, passing the gardens harvested of their summer vegetables. He grumbled about how the deer would stuff their bellies with leftover purple-hull peas. The cypress trees the boys and I had planted as seedlings now stood bushy and tall. Mom's camellias, which she'd planted when we first moved into our home, had bloomed. Now, pink petals lay scattered on the grass.

Two large yellow ribbons remained tied onto the front porch handrails—hung there in David's honor. Shutting my eyes, I forced back tears, reminding myself I wasn't abandoning him by leaving the country.

Mom and Pops were waiting at the terminal to say goodbye. My dad taught the boys to call him Pops when they were toddlers. He said grandpa sounded too old for a young man like him. The lump in my throat grew. Pops, like Mom, didn't ask why we wanted to leave our farm. During their fifty years of marriage, I'd never heard them say the word divorce. They'd be disappointed knowing I wanted to break up my family.

Once we'd checked our luggage, we quickly hugged and said goodbye. At the security gate, my eyes stung and my parents disappeared into the crowded corridor.

Walking through the security gate, Laughlin almost toppled under the weight of his Thomas the Train book bag, which Mom had stuffed with goodies and books. Holding his hand, I followed Mark and Ryyan to the boarding area. While we waited, Laughlin chattered about the plane ride like he was going to the circus—unaware he was moving thousands of miles from home because his mom wanted to divorce his dad.

When the time came to board our plane, my feet moved like they were wading through molasses. I stared at my ticket to our next destination—Los Angeles International Airport. Was it too late to turn around and take my family home? What made me think I could make my marriage work in a foreign country, if I couldn't in Georgia?

Once we landed in Los Angeles, we headed toward our connecting flight to Yokota Airbase in Japan.

After a few minutes, an airline representative appeared and announced a delay in the flight to Yokota. The complaints flew through the waiting area like the overripe tomatoes Mark tossed from the garden.

I suggested we have dinner.

Afterward, Mark and the boys explored the terminal. I needed time alone. With the goodbyes, traveling through airports, and riding on the plane, I hadn't thought about what was happening to my family.

My senior year in college, I interned at a center for troubled teenage boys, where I met Mark. He'd left the military three months earlier and worked there.

One Saturday, I went to the center to pick up papers from my office. Mark working at the front gate, checked my identification. He smiled at me revealing boyish dimples. I melted like strawberry ice-cream on a hot summer's day. We were immediately attracted to each other. Soon after, he asked me out on a date.

After a short courtship, Mark took me to meet his parents. We spent the day riding in his dad's old truck chasing cows through the hay fields, strolling through the woods, where we fished in a pond. Late that evening, Mark proposed while an orange sun sank below the woods.

I said yes, but there was a problem. I had a commitment to the US Army after graduation.

Mark asked Pops if he could marry his only daughter. Pops asked Mark if he was ready to follow me in the military, where I would work long hours away from home. He couldn't expect hot meals and a clean house from me. Mark said he'd experienced military life. He'd been a soldier too.

Mom only saw the love we had for each other and helped me plan a small wedding at the Chapel on Fort Benning. The day after, we loaded up our car with wedding gifts and suitcases and drove from Georgia to Fort Bliss, Texas.

A booming voice over the intercom announced the plane was boarding for Yokota Japan Airbase. Mark and the boys grabbed our luggage. On wobbly legs, I followed my family down the corridor.

CHAPTER 3—RICE PADDY SHORTCUT

After a sixteen-hour flight, we landed at the Yokota Air Base terminal. Mark wore a thin beard, and we all needed a shower and hot meal. In a long line, we joined service members and their families waiting for an airman to check our passports and carry-on bags.

In a corner, barking dogs and meowing cats circled in their cages. While Mark and the boys focused on the dogs, a fresh wave of guilt washed over me.

"Where's our driver?" Mark said, snatching up our luggage from the rotating belt. In all the preparations for leaving, I didn't get the name or even a description of the person meeting us. Waiting at the airport with a husband who didn't want to be in Japan and two tired children wasn't going to be pleasant.

Through sliding glass doors, a tall, wiry, middle-aged man wearing horn-rimmed glasses charged in. "Are you the Smith family?" he said.

"Yes," I replied, smiling with relief.

"I'm Wayne, your driver. Sorry I'm late—traffic," he said, reaching out to shake our hands.

"How'd you know who we were?" I said.

"You're the only family arriving from Georgia with two boys," he said, grinning.

Outside the airport, we followed Wayne through the parking lot as waves of heat rose from the concrete, and the heavy humidity mimicked the hot summer days we left in Georgia. We loaded our luggage into a Toyota minivan.

"So no one sits in my lap," Wayne said, "the Japanese drive on the left."

Mark sat in the passenger seat. The boys and I piled into the back. Wayne started the van and blasted us in all directions with cold air.

"Buckle up," Wayne said. "We have an hour's drive to Atsugi Base."

Wayne pointed toward a three-story brick building. "That's Yokota Navy Exchange. You'll want to come here and purchase your electronic equipment," he said, winking at the boys through the rearview mirror.

Two white-gloved airmen, with rifles slung over their shoulders, waved us through a metal gate topped with barbed wire as we exited the air base.

In Yokota City, Wayne nudged the van onto a narrow street into a slow moving line of cars and buses. A moped whizzed by my window. Pedestrians and bicycle riders raced across the street under a canopy of thick black cables with traffic lights dangling like bulbs on Christmas trees. A train packed with people flashed past.

Our town back home had two red lights, and you only saw pedestrians during a parade. How was I supposed to drive in endless traffic and on the left side of the road?

After the van moved three feet, and studying the trail of cars in his rearview mirror, Wayne said, "We'll never get to Atsugi City in this traffic—time to take a shortcut."

The van veered off the main road, picking up speed. I grabbed the handle above my door and hung on. We veered onto a narrow one-way street and raced up and down hills, past rice paddies, curly-topped houses, and high-rise apartment buildings. We twisted and turned on the narrow roads like a rattlesnake crossing the road. I glanced at the boys—both were asleep. Mark and Wayne were chattering away, as if they were on a Sunday drive down a country road. I closed my eyes, not wanting to witness the head-on crash sure to happen at any moment.

"We're here," Wayne said.

"Where?" I said, peering out the van's windows at tall buildings, shops, apartments, and more thick, dangling black cables.

"Atsugi Naval Air Facility," he said.

After a sharp right turn under a traffic light, the van stopped behind a line of cars waiting to enter another guarded gate. The van's bumper stuck out into the intersection, blocking traffic.

I cringed waiting for honking horns and rude gestures from the other cars, but they never came. Drivers waited patiently for us to move. When we arrived at the gate, airmen checked our passports and waved us through.

Fresh cut lawns, colorful flowers, and cherry trees lined the air base's wide streets. A towering, red, wooden structure, with two curved upper lintels resting on two long wooden posts, stood centered in a roundabout.

"That's Atsugi's torii gate," Wayne said. "Toriis mark the entrances to shrines—places of worship for the Japanese. You'll see them all over Japan."

Further into the base, we drove past football and baseball fields. "Most of the younger sailors play sports when they're not onboard the ship," Wayne said.

"What's the building with the curly top roof?" Mark said.

"The Chapel of the Good Shepherd, our base chapel," Wayne said.

At a four-way intersection, golden arches rose into the sky.

"McDonald's," Laughlin shouted.

"Let's stop and eat," Wayne said, "before I drop you off at the Navy Lodge."

While we ate dinner, Wayne said he was the supply clerk for the school, and because of his driving skills, he also picked up new teachers from the airport. His wife worked for a retired navy man now a realtor, he said, handing me a business card. I quickly tucked the card into my purse. Renting a house would mean moving outside the gate—and driving in nightmare traffic.

Back in the van, we passed a playground before Wayne drove up next a tan, L-shaped stucco building with "Navy Lodge" written in large, fancy letters across the top.

"I have to get back," Wayne said, unloading our suitcases onto a luggage cart. "Your sponsor will call you soon. Everything you need is within walking distance." He joked with the boys a few minutes, waved goodbye, and drove off.

I shivered under the scorching sun watching our traveling partner, who spoke the Japanese language and maneuvered the spider-web streets of Japan, leave us. Laughlin scampered toward the Navy Lodge, while Mark and Ryyan pushed the luggage cart behind him. Gaping at the Navy Lodge, fighting the thought Mark was right and I was wrong about moving to Japan, I picked up my carry-on bag and followed. No car. No home. No family. We were on our own.

CHAPTER 4—THE RED TOP

"How long do we have to live here?" Mark said, glaring at two full-sized beds stuffed into our lodge room.

The boys looked at me, feeling the argument brewing, and darted to their room across from ours. While I checked out the room, Mark took a shower. In addition to the two beds, a miniature kitchen sat toward the back of the room in a corner, with a small, round table and four chairs. A large flat-screen TV sat on a chest of drawers. The bathroom was the size of a closet with a vanity on the outside.

On the far wall, I drew back dark, heavy drapes. Sunlight flooded the room. A few cars sat in the lodge's square-shaped parking lot. At the far corner, a sidewalk led to the chapel. And across the street, a neon sign flashed Parcheesi's Restaurant. Downsizing from our country home wasn't going to be easy, but for two weeks, I could make it work.

The red light flashed on the telephone.

"Hi, this is Tony Robinson, welcome to Japan. Do you need anything?"

"No, thank you," I said, glad to hear from our sponsor. "Wayne did a good job driving us to the lodge."

"Can we meet in the lobby at nine o'clock tomorrow morning? Ms. Phipps wants you both to visit the school for a tour."

"We'll be there," I said.

Late that night in the boys' room, a Japanese Sponge Bob sang loudly on the television screen. The boys were asleep. I picked up wet towels and dirty clothes and turned off the TV on my way out. Back in our room, I unpacked our suitcases. I didn't have time to fret about driving in Japan or living in the lodge. Tomorrow, I needed to make a good impression on my new boss.

The next morning, I left Ryyan a note to take Laughlin to McDonald's for breakfast and the playground. We'd be back before lunch.

Waiting in the lobby for Tony, Mark relaxed on an oversized couch and read a magazine, while I checked the desk for a message from David. Walking back to the couch, I overheard Mark talking.

"We left our farm to come to this crowded country with never-ending traffic and live in a cramped motel room," he said to a young lady sitting next to him, her curly brown hair falling forward as she leaned in to listen.

"Exactly why did you leave your farm?" she said.

"We thought living in Japan would be a great adventure for our boys," I butted in, crossing my arms, glaring at Mark. Before I could find out what else Mark told her, a middle-aged man wearing a baseball cap, shorts, and sneakers rushed through the lodge's sliding glass doors.

"Hi, I'm Tony," he said. "Sorry I'm late. Traffic. I see you've met Yolanda. She's a new teacher, too."

"I've met the Smiths," she said, standing abruptly and tossing us a thin smile. "I'll see you later. I've already gone on the tour." She hurried toward the glass doors.

Before my embarrassment rose to anger, Tony whisked us away from the lodge in the school's van. The last thing I needed was Ms. Phipps to learn she'd hired a couple on the verge of a divorce.

We took a tour of the base on the way to Lanham Elementary. The base formed one large circle starting at McDonald's. At the four-way stop sign, Tony pointed out the base swimming pool, a gym, a commissary where we could purchase food, a clinic, dry cleaners, and post office. We passed a three-story brick building across from the chapel.

"That's the Family Support Center where Sunday school is held and classes for the sailors are taught," Tony said.

Past the Family Support Center was the front gate we'd entered with Wayne. I shuddered, glimpsing the traffic jam outside the gate. Traveling away from the Navy Lodge and the chapel, we drove past several high-rise apartment complexes with sidewalks and flower beds separating them from parking lots. Single family homes nestled against shady trees, shrubs, and flowers, all surrounded by freshly cut grass. Playgrounds dotted the housing area.

"This is the family housing area where our students and their parents live," said Tony, pulling into a parking lot in front of a one-story brick building. "Here we are—Shirley Lanham Elementary School."

A boom rocked the ground, and a white streak crossed the blue sky.

"What's that ?" Mark said, searching the sky.

"A F-18 Hornet jet assigned to the aircraft carrier Kitty Hawk," Tony said, walking toward the school. "You're going to teach that pilot's kids."

At the school's door waited a petite well-dressed lady with a warm smile.

"Hello, I'm Ms. Phipps," she said, shaking our hands. "Welcome to Lanham Elementary. You are now part of our family."

Inside, we followed her down a hallway with shiny floors and children's art decorating the walls into a conference room.

"Atsugi Naval Air Facility is the largest air base in the Pacific and houses the squadrons of Carrier Air Wing 5," Ms. Phipps said, standing beside a large map with dots splattered across a deep blue Pacific Ocean. "Our mission is to support these pilots and sailors by providing their children with a high-quality education. The folder in front of you contains paperwork for obtaining off-base housing and your new driver's licenses. I've scheduled you both to attend driver's class tomorrow. I know you just arrived, but the sooner you get your licenses, the quicker you can settle into a home. School starts in two weeks."

I squirmed in my chair, visualizing crumpled cars and people yelling while I stood in the middle.

"Let me show you around the school. Our teachers are on summer break." Ms. Phipps led us down the hallway and pointed out the kindergarten through third-grade classes, a library, and computer lab. "Grades four through six are outside in a separate building."

Ms. Phipps opened heavy metal doors to exit the building, ushering a burst of warm air into the building. We walked toward a large area where swings, sliding boards, and jungle gyms were arranged on red plastic tiles.

"This is the Red Top, our playground area," Ms. Phipps said. "Teachers and students assemble here in the mornings before classes begin. Now look up," she said, "That's Mt. Fuji, Japan's famous mountain."

In the sky, a gigantic, cone-shaped mass of rock and earth silhouetted against a cloudless blue sky stared down at me. The mountain's unexpected size and beauty pinned my feet to the ground.

"Are you okay?" Mark said, walking away quickly to catch up with Ms. Phipps.

"Sure," I stammered, trailing them, looking back, captivated by the mountain's beauty.

"Here we are—fourth grade," Ms. Phipps said, stopping at a classroom door to a newly constructed two-story brick building. "Mrs. Smith, this is your room," she said, opening the door. "Mr. Thomas's classroom is next door. Mr. Smith and I are headed upstairs."

The spacious classroom was twice the size of my previous schools. A large cabinet stood in the center of the back wall. Two large bulletin boards faced each other on opposite sides of the room. Student desks and chairs were placed in small groups, and a computer center sat in a corner. A large white board was mounted on a front wall.

I relaxed in the high-backed swivel chair at the teacher's desk, smiling as I imagined my students working hard at their desks. Becoming a school teacher was the ideal profession for me after the military. Teaching gave me the opportunity to enjoy summers and holidays with my children. While serving in the army, I missed first steps, first words, and first days of school.

My excitement quickly waned when I remembered I wasn't in Japan only to teach. I was here to fix a marriage most people would've given up on a long time ago. I thought back to Mark's earlier conversation with the young lady in the lobby. Could we work together and teach our students with his negative attitude? I shook off my uneasiness and went upstairs to Mark's classroom.

"What do you think about the school?" I said, scanning Mark's classroom—identical to mine.

"Not bad," he replied, examining a cabinet's content. "Did you notice these classrooms have two bulletin boards? Middle-school teachers don't put up cutesy boards," Mark said, rubbing the back of his neck. "How are we supposed to get our classrooms ready, plan lessons, buy cars, and move into a house before school starts?"

He was right. In the military, I didn't have to set up an office or take my family to work with me.

I arranged books on a shelf, not wanting Mark to see I, too, was overwhelmed. This was not the time to show weakness. If Mark thought I had any doubts about coming, he'd be on the next plane back to Georgia.

"Working together, we can get everything done," I said, "For now, let's get the boys and have lunch."

Back at the lodge, I opened our room door. Both beds were neatly made, white towels were stacked on the shelf above the vanity, and suitcases were tucked neatly into a corner. Ryyan and Laughlin sat in chairs watching television as though someone had dared them to get onto the freshly made beds.

"This is a nice surprise." I said. "What happened?"

"A lady knocked on the door and asked if she could clean the room," Ryyan said.

"Let's eat lunch. Later we can shop at the commissary for dinner," I said.

"Without a car?" Ryyan said.

"Yes. We can walk," I said, replacing my sandals with sneakers.

"Really?"

"Walking will give us an opportunity to see the base and exercise at the same time. Now, let's go," Mark said.

I grabbed my purse and held a smile inside as I followed Mark and the boys out the door. This was the first time in months Mark and I had agreed on something.

CHAPTER 5—SOMEWHERE IN IRAQ

After lunch at Parcheesi, our next stop was the commissary to shop for groceries. Mangos, papaya, Asian pears, a variety of melons, leeks, cabbages, Japanese yams, and bamboo shoots made the produce section resemble an indoor farmers' market. I left Mark in the produce section. The boys started shopping in the cereal and snack aisle, while I shopped for the family's favorite dinner—pasta and meat sauce.

Our buggies were piled high by the time we got to the cash register. When the bagger asked where our car was in the parking lot, Ryyan gave us an I-told-you-so look.

Spaghetti sauce bubbled on the two-burner stove as I prepared my family's first meal away from home. Laughlin blessed the food, prayed for David's safety, and that his grandmother didn't miss him too much. At the end of dinner, laughter burst from around the table when Mark's face puckered sampling the exotic fruits.

Later, Laughlin sat cross-legged on the bed in his pajamas, enchanted by the Japanese cartoon characters chasing each other across the TV screen.

"Hey, guys, time for bed," I said.

"Why do I have to go?" Ryyan said. "I'm in high school now. I shouldn't have a bedtime just because I share a room with a first-grader."

"We're in the lodge for two weeks. In our new house, you'll have your own room."

"When can we visit my new school?"

I started organizing clothes in a suitcase. I didn't want Ryyan to know my apprehension about driving and living outside the gate.

"We have our driver's test tomorrow."

"Great," he said putting on his earphones.

I clicked off the TV.

"Ah, Mommy," Laughlin complained.

"Let's read together," I said, laying back on the bed and pulling him close to me with his favorite book.

Soon, slow breathing replaced, "Read that part again, Mommy."

As I left the boys' room, I noticed one painting above the television. Missing were kindergarten drawings and professional football players' posters on the boys' wall back in Georgia. Was I cheating the boys out of the stable home life I didn't have growing up? Guilt kept finding a back door to make me have second thoughts about leaving our home. We were all together, a family. Nothing else mattered.

Back in our room, Mark sat at the table completing paperwork Ms. Phipps had given us, when the television news caught our attention.

"The death toll in Iraq is climbing," the anchorman said. The footage showed a man and woman dressed in black, wiping their eyes, watching soldiers carrying a coffin draped with an American flag from a plane.

"How will David's unit get in touch with us if something happens?" Mark said, eyes fixed on the screen.

I sensed Mark's barrage of reasons coming on why we shouldn't be in Japan.

"The Army will find us," I muttered, closing my eyes, trying to erase the coffin scene from my mind.

My answer didn't satisfy Mark. We both knew it could take days or weeks for the army to contact a soldier's family. I picked up the base phone book and flipped through the pages.

"The Red Cross," I said, writing down the number.

"What'd you say?" Mark said.

"The Red Cross—they notify service members families when there's an emergency. All military bases have one."

At ten o'clock, I explained to the Red Cross representative why I needed to get in touch with our son. She said giving a soldier an address was not an emergency. Too many priority messages informing next of kin from Iraq were already flooding their office. She took our names and the phone number for Lanham School, but couldn't promise David would receive our message.

I crawled into one of the beds while the news from Iraq blared from the television. The coffin scene tormented me. I turned my back to the TV, not wanting Mark to see my tears.

My eyes opened to a dark room. The only lights were red buttons on the phone sitting on the nightstand. Disoriented, my heart raced. I focused my blurry eyes on the shapes in the darkness. Where and why I was here, came back to me. We'd left our home in Georgia.

I tiptoed across the room and pulled back the curtains. This time no brilliant sunlight, only a parking lot lined with cars. I piled our traveling clothes into my arms and retrieved a travel-sized box of laundry detergent from a suitcase. I crossed the hall and entered the boys' room. Clothes spilled out of open suitcases and dirty ones were tossed next to the bathroom door.

I gathered their clothes, too, and padded my way down the hall to the laundry room. With several washers and dryers available in the early morning hours, I loaded up the machines. At the folding table, next to a large curtainless window in the laundry, I waited for the clothes to dry. Like I'd waited to go home those long days on the missile range in Fort Bliss, Texas.

The only woman inside the missile control center packed with men in McGregor Range, New Mexico, I drove thirty miles before daylight to lead my platoon. No schooling or training could have prepared me for life in the military as a female officer. If I wasn't fighting at work to prove myself, I fought with Mark because I was seldom home. Relief came when I transferred to the Signal Corps in Fort Gordon, Georgia.

In Fort Gordon, life settled down for us with my assignment to train soldiers. Soon David was born, and Mom and Pops got to spoil their first grandchild. After two years, I was assigned to Germany where Ryyan was born. Returning to work was tough after maternity leave. Mark got the boys ready for daycare and dropped them off on his way to work, and I'd rush home late evenings and pick them up. After a few snowy months shuttling the boys to daycare, Mark quit his job and became a stay-at-home dad.

On the balcony of our German high-rise apartment, fireworks exploded and brilliant colors splashed across a winter sky, Mark and I celebrated the New Year. After twelve years in the service, I yearned for a place to call home, so we left the military.

As I was folding clothes in the laundry room, outside the window, a red speck slowly spread into an orange ball against a charcoal sky. At five o'clock in the morning, the Japanese sun lit up the sky.

The rising sun reminded me of our driving class. I picked up our folded laundry and wished driving in Japan were easy as washing clothes.

CHAPTER 6—A SPORTY RED NISSAN

"A written test with a passing score is mandatory to receive your license," our Japanese instructor explained as she passed out papers covered with symbols to the class. "No road test is required with a US license. If you injure a pedestrian, you must go to the hospital every day and take fresh flowers," she added, peering at me.

After two hours lecturing and reviewing road signs, she passed out the tests.

Twenty minutes later, Mark rose and handed the instructor his paper. After a few minutes, she nodded. He smiled at me, leaving the room.

A half hour later, in an empty classroom, I checked over my answers one last time. Hands shaking, I gave my test to the instructor.

"How'd you do?" Mark said, standing outside the classroom door.

"I passed," I said, examining the license permitting me to drive in Japan.

"Great, with a little practice driving, you'll be whizzing around Japan in a few weeks."

I gave Mark a quick smile. We'd be back in Georgia, with the practice I needed, before I drove in Japan.

Sunday morning, as Mark slept, I slipped out of the room to pick up breakfast from McDonald's. On my way back, I glimpsed Yolanda waiting at the elevator. I scurried toward the stairs, hoping she hadn't seen me. But she quickly intercepted me with a smile and an invitation for the family to tour Tokyo with her today. I thought about another day in the lodge and said yes.

"Hey, guys, how would you like to ride the train to Tokyo today?" I said during breakfast.

"Why do you want to go there?" Mark said.

"Yolanda invited us, and Tokyo is one of the largest, most exciting cities in the world," I said, rising from the table, looking for an escape from a room too small for an argument.

"I'll stay," Mark said, picking up the remote.

I tossed breakfast containers into the trash. Mark not spending time with the boys and me was one reason we argued. If our outings didn't involve tractors, automotive shows, gardens, or fishing, he wasn't going.

I quickly stuffed jackets and snacks into a backpack. Mark could stay cooped up in the room.

In the lodge parking lot, in Yolanda's back seat, sat a little girl with curly black hair and baby-doll eyes clutching a pink Little Mermaid backpack.

"This is my daughter, Mickey. She starts kindergarten this year," Yolanda said.

The boys hopped into the car next to Mickey's car seat and buckled up. Before we drove out the front gate, giggles rose from the back seat.

Yolanda maneuvered though the early-morning traffic toward the train station while I hugged the passenger-side door. She asked me when we planned to buy a car. I mumbled, "We're looking."

Zama Train Station looked like an ant farm with people flowing in and out. I grasped Laughlin's hand and followed Yolanda's red jacket and Mickey's pink backpack through a maze of electronic gates. On the platform, we joined commuters in the packed compartment of the train. After several stops, more people pushed their way in. At the next stop, Yolanda signaled us to follow her.

After climbing a steep staircase at Shinjuku Station in Tokyo, we emerged from underground into masses of people. Japanese youths wore stylish clothes and sported spiked purple and red hair. Men in tailored blue and black suits carrying briefcases rushed past us through the crowd. Women in stylish skirts and jackets with large designer handbags looped over their shoulders sauntered along in their pointed-toe, high-heeled shoes.

At the Ginza—a swanky shopping district in downtown Tokyo—we strolled past designer clothing stores and novelty shops. Locals and tourists sipped tea and coffee in glass-faced restaurants. We explored shops in back alleys and tucked under staircases. Midday, the children complained they were hungry.

On the city's outskirts, a massive torii gate towered at the Meiji Shrine entrance. Inside, a forest surrounded the shrine—the perfect place for a picnic.

Laughlin and Mickey chased each other on the playground after lunch, while Yolanda and I relaxed on a bench under a cluster of cherry trees. Ryyan wandered toward the Meiji Shrine temple, where groups of people quietly milled around gray, billowing smoke rising from a huge, black pot.

"I've found an apartment, and we're moving out of the lodge on Monday," Yolanda said, placing crumpled sandwich wrappings into a bag.

I admired Yolanda's independence—moving to a foreign country with her daughter, driving in the crazy traffic, and now moving into her own place.

"I'm sorry about butting in on your conversation with Mark the other day," I told her.

"I understand," Yolanda said. "He told me about David."

I dropped my head.

"I'm sorry," Yolanda said—her fingers lightly touched my hand.

"I don't know where he is in Iraq, and ..." Yolanda waited for me to finish, but I couldn't tell her my marriage was in trouble, and I thought moving to Japan would help us heal. Now, I thought maybe leaving wasn't a good idea.

"Look, Mom," Ryyan said, pointing toward the temple's entrance.

A Japanese bride in a white kimono, her silky, black hair pulled up under an elegant hair piece, strolled next to her groom while family and friends trailed behind. Remembering the excitement of my wedding day, I prayed their commitment to each other would weather the seasons of a long marriage.

"How was your trip?" Mark said, as Laughlin ran into the room and jumped on the bed.

"The train was really fast," Laughlin said.

"Thousands of people shopping in one place," Ryyan said.

"I found a car while you guys were sightseeing—a red, four-door Nissan parked at the baseball field with a For Sale sign in the window."

"Now we can visit my school," Ryyan said.

"Let's get the motor checked out first. I've already called the owner. We can test-drive the car tomorrow."

With the television off, fast trains, expensive stores, and a red Nissan dominated our evening conversation.

Monday morning, Mark merged the Nissan into traffic traveling toward Zama American High School. The morning rush hour had whittled down to a few cars and buses. Along the sidewalk, a group of elementary school children, wearing their yellow beanie hats, traipsed behind an adult holding up a triangular flag. They looked like ducklings following a mama duck. Mark drove through the city like a seasoned driver while I navigated, using Tony's directions to the high school located on Zama Army Base.

I eased back into my seat, taking in the busy city as we passed storefronts familiar from traveling with Wayne our first day in Japan. After several turns, we drove up a steep hill. Below sat Zama Army Base and a familiar sight, soldiers guarding a gate.

Driving through the base, I became an army brat again. The buildings were all the same color. The grass was cut short without a blade growing between the cracks in the sidewalk. No trash could be seen on the lawns or the streets. Replicas of tanks and aircraft were strategically placed along the main road—a reminder service members fight on the ground and in the air.

We turned down a street with a sign pointing to Zama High School. The three-story building was huge compared to Ryyan's school in Georgia. A Trojan mascot stood proudly in the lobby, and a display case stuffed with trophies lined the walls.

The counselor greeted us with a smile inside her office.

"I see you did well scholastically at your last school and also played football," she said, looking at Ryyan's records. "A foreign language requirement of three years is required for high school graduation. You can choose Spanish or Japanese," she said.

Before Ryyan could say Spanish, I said, "Japanese. Someone in our house needs to speak the language."

Ryyan frowned.

"Do you like to read?" the counselor said.

He nodded.

"Good," she said, and handed him Hiroshima by John Hersey. "This is a ninth-grade reading requirement. You have the first semester to finish reading the book and to write a report."

"High school's tougher than I thought," Ryyan said.

The counselor gave us a quick school tour and dropped us off in the gym after introducing us to the football coach.

"Welcome to Zama High," a large, red-faced man with a Santa Claus beard said, reaching out to shake Ryyan's hand. "I hear you're not only interested in football, but a good student too. What position do you play?" he asked, studying Ryyan's body.

"Running back."

"Practice starts the first day of school. We have a bus pick up players at the lodge. Can I count on you joining the team?"

"Sure, Coach."

I beamed, listening to Ryyan, the coach, and Mark talk about winning football teams. Friday night football games always brought us together. Slowly, some guilt I'd carried about moving to Japan lifted.

Back at the lodge, I pulled out the realtor's business card Wayne had given me and dialed the number. I needed to find a home for my family.

"Mr. Dodson has an opening to show houses tomorrow," Waynes's wife said. "He'll pick up your family outside the lodge in the morning."

CHAPTER 7—A FIVE-SPEED TOILET

The next morning, we stood under the Lodge's canopy watching rain pour from cloudy skies. A minivan pulled up. A man with short-cropped hair and olive skin motioned us into the van. We dashed the short distance through the rain. Mark slid into the passenger seat, and the boys and I squeezed into the back.

"Good morning." Mr. Dodson said. "The monsoons are early. Where are you folks from?"

"Sparta, Georgia," Mark said.

"Like In the Heat of the Night?" Mr. Dodson said, tipping his head to the side.

"No, that's a fictitious town." Mark said as though Mr. Dodson should've known. "We live on a farm my family has owned for three generations." He proceeded to give Mr. Dodson the family history, all while complaining about the traffic and people jammed onto a tiny island. I cleared my throat. Mr. Dodson peeked at me through the rearview mirror. I gave him a half-smile.

"Well," Mr. Dodson interjected, "considering what you left behind, the family will need a large house. I have a couple available."

We traveled with the traffic toward Zama City, passing people donning rain suits and some even holding umbrellas while riding their bikes. Mr. Dodson shot the van across a narrow street, dodged fast-moving traffic, and turned into a gravel parking lot. When we got out of the van, the pouring rain had become a sprinkle. Mr. Dodson pointed to a house on the other side of the traffic-laden street.

"Let's go," he said, dashing across the busy street.

Mark and Ryyan sprinted after him. Grabbing Laughlin's hand, I darted behind them. Speeding traffic hemmed us against the house's front door. When Mr. Dodson opened the door, we spilled into a small brick foyer. Mark and Ryyan stepped onto the shiny, dark wood floors flowing throughout the house.

"Wait," Mr. Dodson shouted. "You can't walk on the floor with your shoes on. The Japanese don't wear shoes inside the house." Taking off his shoes, he placed them neatly inside a cabinet in the foyer. Mark and Ryyan, surprised by the request, followed suit. I smiled inside. No more grimy shoes tracking dirt through the house.

On the first floor, we walked through a room large enough for the family. Next to it was a kitchen and a bathroom. Upstairs were four small bedrooms and a bathroom. Back downstairs, I peeked out the tiny window in the front door. Cars, mopeds, and buses swooshed by. Mark and I agreed if we lived here, Laughlin could never go outside.

"I have another house to show you close to Zama High School. Your son can ride a bike to school." Mr. Dodson said. The van snaked through Zama City's narrow streets and turned at a Japanese middle school sitting on the corner. Below the school, cherry trees surrounded a park with a playground.

Past the park, a neighborhood appeared. Two-story houses, built close together and painted in rainbow colors, looked like nesting boxes in a chicken coop,. Futons and laundry hung on narrow balcony railings, and potted flowers clustered in doorways. Turning the van into a cul-de-sac, Mr. Dodson drove past a row of houses, stopped next to a narrow, two-story, sky-blue house, and backed into the driveway

"This is it," he said.

"Looks like a dollhouse," I said, squeezing out the van, careful not to hit the neighbor's car.

"We're awfully close to the house next door ... the Akimotos," Mark said, reading a brass nameplate on the front door.

"Neighborhoods are like this in the city," Mr. Dodson said. "Don't forget to bring each neighbor a gift—a Japanese custom."

Mark and I glanced at each other.

"We have two cars. If we decide to live here, where will we park the other car?" Mark said.

"There's a gravel parking lot for extra parking space before you enter the neighborhood."

Mr. Dodson opened the door. As we entered the foyer, we remembered to take off our shoes.

In the hallway, I ran my hands along wallpaper etched with long-legged cranes and cherry blossoms. A wooden staircase led to three bedrooms and a closet size bathroom. In the master bedroom, a narrow balcony provided a view of rooftops and a beautiful mountain range.

Downstairs, a modest-sized kitchen contained a sink and a stovetop. "Where's the oven?" Mark said.

Mr. Dodson pulled out a rack, large enough for two slices of toast, from under the stovetop.

"You can't cook a turkey in there," Mark said, peering inside the narrow space.

"That's for broiling fish. The Japanese don't cook full-course meals. You can get an oven along with your furniture from the housing department on the Navy base," Mr. Dodson said. The laundry room, with a shower and sink, was attached to the kitchen.

We stood in a family room where double glass doors opened onto a mini patio and a patch of grass. While Mr. Dodson and Mark discussed how to use the heating and cooling systems in the house, I searched for storage space.

The house was half the size of our home in Georgia, I'd have to share a bathroom with the guys—and if the neighbor's curtains were up, I would be able to see inside their house.

"Dad and Mom, come here," Ryyan said. We all crammed into the downstairs bathroom. While Laughlin pushed buttons on the toilet, water sprayed and spiraled upward inside the commode.

"That's what I call a five-speed toilet," Mr. Dodson said. Grinning and pointing to the buttons on the toilet, he demonstrated the different features like a car salesman. "With the heated seat, this will become the most popular place in the house this winter."

"What do you think?" I said to Mark.

"We'll take it," he said, experimenting with the buttons on the toilet.

"There's one problem," Mr. Dodson said. "The house won't be available for two weeks."

"Oh, no—two weeks," I said. The lodge room was shrinking, and with school starting soon, we needed a home. Although the house was small, a park sat nearby and there was no speeding traffic. I'd wait.

CHAPTER 8—LANHAM SCHOOL BELL RINGS

With school starting in a week, Ms. Phipps summoned all teachers to the school's library for a meet-and-greet. I fidgeted with my pencil and notepad. Were the other new teachers nervous like me , starting the school year teaching in a foreign country.

After going over the teachers' handbook, Ms. Phipps asked us to introduce ourselves.

A slender, middle-aged man with short blond hair stood.

"My name is Douglas Thomas," he said softly, his serious blue eyes peering through metal-framed glasses. "I've taught in Japan for twenty years, and I like teaching fourth-grade social studies," he said, quickly taking his seat.

Ms. Phipps told us Doug had failed to mention he'd taught at Lanham longer than any other faculty member, had traveled extensively throughout Japan, and was fluent in Japanese. If we had questions about living and traveling in Japan, ask Mr. Thomas.

After the meeting, Mark and I stopped by Doug's classroom. Inside, stacked textbooks stood in a corner, world maps lined the walls, and students' artwork hung from the ceiling. Doug was busy loading books onto a cart and transporting them across the room to a bookshelf.

"Hello," he said, stopping for a minute to shake both our hands. "The days before school starts get really busy around here. Let me know if you need anything."

"I feel like a fish out of water in this elementary school," Mark said, sitting at a student desk in his classroom. "Where do we start?"

I didn't want to tell Mark how nervous I felt teaching overseas. I was a small-town, country teacher.

"Our bulletin boards need decorating. Pull everything out of the cabinets, and I'll do the same, and we'll get started," I said, returning to my classroom.

Doug came into my room carrying poster boards while I looked through the large cabinets for bulletin board materials.

"I thought you and Mark might need these to help decorate your rooms."

"Thanks," I said.

"I'm sorry I didn't have time to speak with you and Mark earlier," he said. "All of my fourth grade team left this year. I had gotten comfortable working with them. So, I'm starting all over again."

"I understand. I left a school system where teachers didn't stay more than a year. They were young and didn't like working in a small country town. Change is good sometimes, and I'm looking forward to working with both you and Mark this year."

"This is your first time working with your husband?"

"Yes, and his first year working in an elementary school. He's anxious about teaching nine-year-olds."

"He sure doesn't look it."

"Oh, he's a country boy. I'm the only person he'll let see him sweat."

A smile crossed Doug's face. "Let me know if you need any help. I normally work late to avoid traffic."

Mark and I worked through the morning. Between the school's supply room, Doug's contributions, and posters we found in the closets, we managed to decorate the bulletin boards in both Mark's classroom and mine.

Mark helped in my classroom, placing math and science textbooks on students' desks and arranging tables and chairs. As Mark worked, I remembered how excited he was returning to college and obtaining a degree in education. While we traveled in the military, Mark enrolled in college classes, but never had time to complete a degree. When we returned to Georgia, he found an opportunity.

Mark loved teaching. If he wasn't showing the boys how to rebuild an engine, he was in the garden, explaining to them how a bee pollinates vegetables.

I longed to tell Mark how happy I was he'd come to Japan, and that I wanted our marriage to get better. But with my heart tender from years of arguments and distancing ourselves from each other, I couldn't. Right now, holding onto my pain felt safer. Instead, I said goodbye when he returned to his classroom.

The phone rang in my classroom. Ms. Phipps wanted me in her office immediately. What could have happened? Was I in trouble already?

Rushing there, I found only Mark, who stood by her desk, talking on the phone. He said David. I leaped across the room and joined the conversation, ear to ear we talked and listened as Mark held the phone between us.

David said he got the Red Cross message. He travels across the desert repairing vehicles, which makes contacting us difficult. He spoke to Gma whenever he had a chance to call. After a quick "I love you, and tell my brothers hello," David hung up.

Mark slowly placed the phone onto the receiver and wrapped his arms around me. I didn't pull away like I had many times before. I buried my face in his shoulder and wept for David and a marriage I wasn't sure could be saved.

We spent the next two days planning lessons, writing name tags for students' desks, and familiarizing ourselves with the Department of Defense Curriculum. Both Tony and Doug helped us navigate living on the base and getting to know our colleagues. Ms. Phipps checked on us to ensure we had everything we needed at the lodge and for our classrooms. We worked late into the evenings, making last-minute touches to our rooms and lesson plans right up until the day before school started.

Mark and I went over our lesson plans while lying in bed the night before the first day of school. He soon fell asleep, but I lay awake, unsettled by Mark's words to Yolanda and Mr. Dodson regarding his discontent about living in Japan. Our life here was in motion now—too late to say I'd made a mistake coming to Japan.

I removed a platter of bacon, eggs, and toast from the oven when Ryyan entered our lodge room.

"Good morning. Sit down and eat," I said, eyeing his jeans, shirt, and sneakers and pushing back tears. I missed the starched white button-down shirt, slacks, polished shoes, and tie Mark helped him with on the first day of school.

"I'm not hungry. I just want to go downstairs and catch the bus," Ryyan said, slinging his book bag onto his shoulder.

"You're thirty minutes early."

"I'll miss the bus."

"Okay, but at least take a few bites."

Ryyan stood nibbling on a breakfast sandwich while Mark lectured him on setting high goals and starting off with an "A" attitude. Ryyan grunted something about hearing this speech every year and said goodbye.

Preparing for the school day to begin, I studied student names on my class roster at my desk while Laughlin stood beside me, coloring.

"Mommy, how do I get to my class?"

I looked up. His fresh haircut and chubby cheeks made him look younger than six.

"We visited your classroom yesterday, and met your teacher."

"I know, but I forgot," he said, tears pooling in his brown eyes.

In Georgia, Laughlin's class was down the hall from me, and I saw him throughout the day. Now, he'd be located in another part of the school—I'd not see him all day.

I walked around the desk, knelt, and enclosed him in my arms.

"You'll be fine. Your teacher will show you."

"What's up?" Mark said, entering the room.

"Going over the day with Laughlin." I said, blinking back tears.

"Time to go," Mark said, ruffling Laughlin's hair.

Mt. Fuji, coned peak jutting into a clear sky, loomed above the Red Top, watching over swarming children, parents, and teachers like a member of the Welcome Back to School Committee. Teachers held up signs with their names and children gathered around them. I found Laughlin's teacher on the Red Top, gave him another quick hug, and joined Mark and Doug in the fourth-grade area.

Slowly, children sporting fresh haircuts, ponytails, and book bags gathered behind me. Some wore nervous smiles, others tugged at new school clothes. My stomach fluttered. I too was nervous and excited about the first day of school.

Service members saluted and civilians placed hands over their hearts as the national anthem played over the intercom. A large American flag waved gently, rising up a pole into the air. Ms. Phipps, standing on a platform, spoke through a bullhorn welcoming parents, students, and teachers back to school. She rang a bell, officially starting the school year.

In the classroom, students quickly located their names on desks. Several parents had followed us from the Red Top and now stood in the back of the room. I stuttered out my introduction to the class as parents smiled. One parent made a light-hearted joke about y'all in the South. While I called the class roll, parents eased from the room. I breathed a sigh of relief. I had passed the good teacher test.

The first day went by smoothly. With my 'get-to-know you' activities, I discovered my students were bright, inquisitive, and well-traveled. They had fun learning I lived on a farm, and Mr. Smith, their math and science teacher, was my husband. After introductions, we organized school supplies and covered class rules and routines. Performing these activities for three classes, the first day went by quickly.

When the last bell rang, Laughlin burst into my classroom, dropped his book bag, and rattled on about his new friends, his pretty teacher, and how he didn't have homework the first day. He ran back out the door, saying his friends were waiting on the Red Top.

While Laughlin played, I walked to the housing office to order furniture and appliances for our new home. Posted on their bulletin board was a flyer with a picture of a two-door metallic green Nissan hatchback. The caption below read, Ready for sale, great for narrow Japanese roads. I went to Mark's classroom with the flyer.

"We have smart students," I said.

"They know a lot for little kids," Mark said, posting student work on his bulletin boards.

"I found this in the housing office."

"Looks like a nice car. Can you manage driving off base?"

"The only way I'll know is to try," I said, rubbing goosebumps on my arms.

CHAPTER 9—JAPANESE DRIVING 101

"How was the first day?" I asked, as Ryyan dropped his muddy football uniform at the door.

"Different from my old school. The guys wear long hair, and the seniors don't have to shave."

"What about football?" I said, stirring vegetables into chicken for dinner.

"The coach says our first game is Friday at Yokota Air Base."

I stopped stirring. Yokota City—the place with the horrific traffic. In the years the boys had played football, Mark or I had attended their games.

"It's okay if you and Dad can't come. There'll be more games this year," Ryyan said.

My shoulders sagged with relief.

"I found a car today."

"You did?" Ryyan said, raiding the tiny refrigerator for snacks.

"A Nissan. We have a test-drive after dinner."

"Neat, two cars in one week," he said, grinning.

After dinner, I greeted an older gentleman who stood next to the Nissan Hatchback at the lodge's parking lot. He said the March belonged to his wife. They were returning to the US. He'd sold his car.

I inspected the March. The four doors were great for the boys, and the hatchback would hold several grocery bags or sports equipment. The interior looked new. Seat covers would protect it from spilled soda or ketchup-covered fries. While the owner and Mark discussed the price, I opened the car door and sat down in the driver's seat.

The owner handed me the key and told me to take a test-drive. His wife had needed time getting comfortable driving on the left side. Mark and the boys piled in.

I grabbed the wheel with both hands and sat up straight like a board. I turned the key in the ignition and let the motor run.

"Come on, Mom, you can do this," Ryyan said from the back seat.

I gently pressed my foot on the gas pedal, crept out the parking lot, and pulled into the left-hand lane.

"Good, you remembered," Mark said.

I pulled up to the four-way stop sign next to McDonalds and stopped. Driving forward, I slammed on the brakes when a man stepped out into the crosswalk.

"Not so hard," Mark said, adjusting his seatbelt. "Turn right."

I instinctively turned into the right lane.

"Remember what side you're supposed to drive on," he warned.

I jerked back into the left lane. Sweat dripped down my back even with the air conditioner on full blast. I picked up speed passing the lodge. When I drove past a military police car, the officer glanced at me—my death grip on the steering wheel giving me away as a first-time driver.

The front gate loomed ahead. I quickly turned down a side street and pulled over. I rested my forehead on the steering wheel. If I couldn't drive on base—with its wide streets and no traffic—how was I going to drive on the congested streets of Japan? Mark chauffeuring me everywhere was not an option.

"What's wrong, Mommy?" Laughlin said.

"I can't drive outside the gate."

"Yes, you can," he whined.

"I need more practice."

"You'd better hurry up," Mark said. "We're moving soon."

Friday morning, Ryyan reminded me of his football game in Yokota. After school, I packed suitcases in our room to prepare for the move, and Mark spent time with Laughlin in the boys' room.

Tired from working and packing, I lay on the bed. A ringing phone woke me up.

"Mom," Ryyan said.

"Are you okay?" I said sitting up, walking to the window and pulling back the drapes, to a lighted parking lot filled with cars.

"No, I'm at school with the coach, waiting for a ride. The buses don't run on game days. Tell Dad to hurry and pick me up. I know the coach wants to go home."

I peeked into the boys' room. Mark and Laughlin were asleep. The drive to Zama City took twenty minutes with no traffic. Ryyan and the coach waiting in a parking lot after a long day at school and a football game made me grab the keys to the March. I hurried outside into the muggy night air.

My car sat in the parking lot, untouched, where I'd left it after the test-drive. I fastened my seat belt, said a quick prayer, and reminded myself to think left. I pulled out onto the wide base road and headed toward the gate.

I forced a smile as the guards waved me through, easing past the traffic light. Thankfully, only a few vehicles and pedestrians occupied the usually busy streets. No flying trains crammed with people crossed the curvy roads, no stop and go traffic under red lights.

A car's headlights raced toward me from the other lane. "Stay in your lane. You can do this," I said outloud. The headlights passed. I exhaled.

A large truck barreled head-on into my lane. I gripped the steering wheel, leaned backward, waiting on the impact, the driver quickly turned back into his lane.

When the middle school at the corner of our new neighborhood came into view, I loosened my grip on the steering wheel. The car's engine groaned as it climbed the steep hill to Zama Base. At the top, I cruised toward the welcoming lights.

I shouted when I saw Ryyan and his coach in the parking lot. Hopping into the car, Ryyan gave me a high five. "Good job, Mom. I knew you could do it."

I thanked the coach and fell back into the seat. With all the adjustments I'd had to make in coming to Japan, now at least I could drive.

One day after school, I worked at my desk on lesson plans. With the windows open wide, a breeze carried a hint of fall into my classroom. As I leaned back in my chair, the floor slowly rose, pushing me upward like a rolling wave on the sea, depositing me back down to the floor.

I stood abruptly and held onto my desk. The wave rose again— lifting me up. When the ground stopped moving, I ran outside. The Red Top—silence.

Hurrying to Doug's room, I peeked through the window. He sat at the desk grading a stack of papers. I burst into his room, and grabbed the doorknob, trying to steady my weak knees.

"Did you feel that?" I said,

"The earthquake?" he said, looking up.

"Earthquake?"

"Yes. We have tremors all the time. Since I've been in this part of Japan, we haven't experienced an earthquake powerful enough to cause damage or injury," he said. "Don't fear—we have earthquake drills at school."

"What if I'm at home?"

"Follow your neighbors," he said nonchalantly. "They'll lead you to the earthquake shelter." He went back to grading papers.

Mark came dashing down the stairs.

"Did you feel the ground moving?" he said, eyes wide breathing hard.

"Yeah. Doug said it was an earthquake."

"Where's Laughlin?"

"I thought he was with you."

"He left my room."

We both searched an empty Red Top.

"Let's check the playgrounds," I said my heart racing.

Mark and I went in different directions.

Shouting Laughlin's name. I circled the school and meet back up with Mark.

"I didn't see him. Let's get in the car and drive around," Mark said.

"Could Laughlin walk out the gate without the airman seeing him?" I said.

"Don't even think about it," Mark said, turning before we drove out the gate. Now after dinnertime, the playgrounds were packed with children. My eyes ached searching for Laughlin. Where could he be?

"Let's check back at the school," Mark said. "We'll contact the Navy police to help us search."

My stomach churned thinking the worst possible reasons we couldn't find Laughlin. Driving past the playground near the Navy Lodge, I spotted Laughlin's red shirt he wore to school. Mark pulled the car over. I jumped out and ran toward Laughlin.

"Why did you leave the school?" I said, picking him up, kissing his red, sweaty cheeks.

"I wanted to play at the Pirate Park, Mommy. Am I in trouble?" he said, bottom lip trembling.

"No sweetheart, but next time, ask Dad or me to take you," I said, smiling to keep us both from crying.

We had a week left in the lodge. Between an earthquake and a lost child, I wasn't sure I'd make it.

CHAPTER 10—3-CHOME MIDORIGAOKA

On moving day, Mark's Nissan, jammed with suitcases and a new bicycle in the trunk for Ryyan, left the Navy Lodge for 3-Chome Midorigaoka, our new home. I stayed behind to check out of the lodge. Although I would miss living on base where everything was convenient, I would not miss living and taking care of my family in two rooms. By noon, pedestrians and traffic packed the roads. Picking up Ryyan at Zama Base had boosted my confidence, but I wasn't eager to drive in the heavy Japanese traffic.

Backing into our driveway, I spied Mark in the rearview mirror, leaning against a brick wall, smiling and gesturing to an elderly Japanese lady.

"What took you so long?" he said, waving goodbye to her, strolling toward the car.

"Traffic. Who's the lady?" I said, gathering boxes of dishes and cookware I'd purchased from the Home Store on base.

"That's one of our neighbors. She lives with her daughter and son-in-law." he said, pulling suitcases from the hatchback.

"Does she speak English?"

"Some. We used hand signals. I told her we're from Georgia," Mark said, walking toward the house.

How do you hand gesture 'Georgia' in Japanese?

Inside our new home, our household goods had arrived from Georgia. A refrigerator, microwave, and table with chairs had been delivered by the housing department. Tucked in the corner, next to the range top stood a compact oven— large enough to roast a small turkey. In the shower room, a compact stacked washer and dryer now occupied one corner. Across the hall in the family room, couches, end tables with lamps, and a chair made the room feel cozy. Upstairs, beds, nightstands, and chests of drawers filled each room.

The boys would soon arrive home from school. Excited, I quickly unpacked our boxes from Georgia. I wanted our new house to feel like home.

After dinner, we went out to meet our new neighbors. Ryyan helped us practice saying, "Hello, we are the Smith family" in Japanese.

Mark suggested we start with the neighbor he'd already met.

Sautéed scallions, cabbage, and ginger lingered in the warm night air as we huddled together on their doorstep. Mark knocked while I clutched gift bags stuffed with miniature chocolates, hand towels, and a greeting card.

A young Japanese woman opened the door. Seeing her, I forgot the greeting we'd rehearsed, but managed to shove a bag toward her.

She said something in Japanese over her shoulder, and a young man joined her. The older lady, who had spoken to Mark earlier, entered the room carrying a chubby-cheeked baby. A wisp of black hair pointed up on his bald, baby head. She smiled at the young couple and said in English, "The Smith family from Georgia."

They all bowed low saying, "arigato gozaimasu." We stood smiling at each other. "Arigato gozaimasu means thank you in Japanese," Ryyan said. Bowing, we backed out the doorway.

The next family spoke enough English our awful Japanese didn't offend them. Our Japanese improved visiting our other neighbors. Greeting us with smiles, they accepted our gift bags, bowed and said, "arigato gozaimasu."

With one gift bag left, we returned home and to our next-door neighbors, the Akimotos. Coming from their home, classical piano music floated on the evening air. Mark knocked. The music stopped. A middle-aged Japanese man opened the door.

"Good evening," he said in English. A lady with a porcelain doll's beauty appeared beside him along with two little girls, their long black ponytails swinging in the air, turning to each other giggling at Laughlin. Behind them sat a huge cat blinking at us. Masato introduced himself, his wife Mewa, and daughters. Again, accepting the gift bag, Masato and his family bowed several times. We bowed the short distance between our houses to our door.

Inside our home, I rested against the door, exhausted from the bowing and the hike around the neighborhood. However, meeting our neighbors was worth the work. Mr. Dodson would be proud. We had given each neighbors a gift.

Later, Ryyan complained the house was too quiet without a television. I relished the silence after weeks in the lodge fighting to keep the television off, but I needed to keep up with the news from Iraq. I gave in, promising the boys a trip to Yokota Air Base to shop for a TV.

At bedtime, Laughlin fell asleep in his room—now decorated with toys and posters from his bedroom in Georgia—as I read his favorite book. Ryyan lay sprawled on the bed asleep in his room.

With Mark sleeping soundly in our bedroom, I stepped outside onto our tiny balcony, and hunted for stars hidden behind city lights. What did David's sky look like in Iraq? I wanted him here in Japan with me—with his family.

Stepping back inside, I slipped into bed. My moving day stress melted into the fresh linen sheets.

"Mommy, can I get in bed with you?" Laughlin whispered, standing in our bedroom door. I took his hand and led him back to his room.

"Oh, sweetheart, the bed's too small."

"I can't sleep by myself," Laughlin whimpered. "There's a cat in my room."

We looked out his curtainless window— there, perched on the Akimoto's sill, was the cat I'd seen earlier—inspecting us with wide green eyes. The fat calico wasn't like the cuddly tabby kittens Laughlin played with in the barn.

"Okay. Get into your bed," I said.

"Promise not to leave, Mommy?" he said, eyes moist from a long day and scary cat.

"I'll stay," I said, bending over to kiss his forehead.

Laughlin's soft breathing soon filled the room. The cat crawled away from the window. I stopped at Laughlin's bedroom door, on my way to the comfortable bed waiting for me. I turned around and crawled into the other twin bed. After all, I was the reason Laughlin wasn't sleeping in own his bed back in Georgia.

CHAPTER 11—LANDMARKS

Monday after school, I walked into Tony's classroom.

"How's your new home?" he said, cleaning off his whiteboard.

"Nice, and we have neighbors who speak some English," I said, admiring his first-graders' artwork posted on the walls.

"That's a bonus in a Japanese neighborhood," he said.

"We need to do some shopping at Yokota Air Base this weekend. Mark needs directions."

"Your family's venturing out is good. Most Americans hang around the base, when Japan's beautiful cities are right outside the gate." He drew a map with landmarks. "Remember to leave before the traffic picks up. Traffic is heavy on the weekends. Do you have a cell phone?"

"No, I haven't had time to get one."

"Make time. You'll need one."

Taking Tony's advice, we left early. The traffic flowed steadily, giving Mark the opportunity to show off the Nissan's fast engine on the four-lane highway to Yokota City.

The base's familiar high fence, topped with barbed wire, emerged in the center of the city. Since our arrival in August, Mark and I had moved into our new home, purchased cars, and started new jobs. Working together as a team didn't allow us time to criticize each other or argue about petty things.

The base exchange resembled a three-floor shopping mall in the US, equipped with escalators and two food courts. On the second floor were televisions, video cameras, sound systems, and anything my technology-starved guys craved.

I quickly went to the first floor to shop for curtains to hide the Akimoto's cat. An hour later, I checked the time. I calculated, even taking time for lunch, we could beat the evening traffic.

Returning upstairs, I found Mark and the boys at a cash register with two shopping carts stuffed with large boxes.

We stopped for lunch at the food court. The boys teased about who'd win the first game on their new system. Mark said how antiquated our computer was in Georgia compared to the new one. I beamed, remembering how many weekends I wanted us to come together like this as a family.

As we left the exchange, the black, shiny paint and silver chrome of a Harley-Davidson at the bottom of the escalator pulled Mark's and the boys' attention like a magnet.

Mark's eyes glistened as he ran his hand over the engine, and the boys made revving sounds, squeezing the handlebars. Mark talked about owning a motorcycle one day. Having children and buying a home made a motorcycle a want not a need.

While they marveled at the motorcycle, I reached for the price tag attached to the black leather seat and gasped. The cost could buy a midsize car. I quickly reminded them of the mounting traffic.

Mark packed boxes in the trunk. The boys were asleep before we left the base.

"Does this place look familiar?" Mark said. "We should see signs with Zama City on them by now."

Half asleep, I sat up.

"This isn't the way we came," I said, checking the map for landmarks.

Maneuvering around traffic, Mark turned onto a side street. "This looks like the shortcut Wayne took us through, and the sign says Zama City," he said.

We drove on. The traffic had engulfed the Nissan like a swarm of gnats.

"Maybe we need to stop and ask for directions," I said.

"No, let's drive a little farther," Mark said, eyes fixed on the traffic ahead.

After driving up and down the same street twice, Mark agreed to pull into a gas station. An attendant quickly ran up to the car window.

"We're lost," I said, "and need directions to Zama City."

Smiling, he pointed to a street sign in front of the station.

"Which way?" I said.

"No English," he said, bowing quickly backing away from the car.

My eyes burned, scanning the long chain of cars while Mark inched back into traffic. The sun sank into the ground and landmarks faded into the darkness.

"Are we home yet?" Ryyan said, stirring in the backseat.

"No, son, we took a wrong turn," Mark said, his jaw clenched.

"Mark, let me drive. You've been driving for hours."

"No, I can find the way back. I'm not losing my place in this traffic."

I wanted to lash back, calling him stubborn, but I didn't want to fight. The boys were in the car, and I'd promised myself I wouldn't fight around them anymore.

"Mommy, are we lost? I have to go to the bathroom." Laughlin whimpered.

"Dad, I know where we are," Ryyan said. "The bus came this way after a football game. Turn left at the next traffic light."

Following Ryyan's directions, we entered Zama City, and after several familiar landmarks, we were backing into our driveway. The boys jumped out the car and ran inside.

"That's my last trip," Mark said, slamming the car door, carrying a TV box into the house.

I stepped out the car, hoping Mark didn't mean what he said. Legs numb from the long ride, I trudged toward the door. I glimpsed someone on the Akimoto's porch watering plants. Mewa waved. Embarrassment grew inside me like weeds in a garden. She'd witnessed Mark's outburst. There went our image of the quiet, wholesome family from America. I waved back.

CHAPTER 12—CHAPEL OF THE GOOD SHEPHERD

I woke up with a heavy heart on Sunday morning. We had not attended church since arriving in Japan. I got dressed and roused the boys. While I prepared breakfast, Mark stood in the family room among computer boxes, reading instructions.

"Where are you going?"

"The Chapel of the Good Shepherd on Atsugi Base."

"After yesterday?"

"I know how to get there. Are you coming?" I said through tight lips.

"No, I'll stay here and finish hooking up the computer."

I wasn't surprised. Mark and I had stopped going to church together a long time ago. We'd allowed our dissatisfaction with each other to seep into the one place we could find forgiveness. Sitting in church together pretending to be a happy couple was unbearable.

"Why does Dad always get to stay home?" Ryyan said, hunched down in the car on our way to church. I quickly backed out of the driveway. Mark was supposed to be the Christian leader in our home. I was tired of fussing at the boys making them go to church.

I missed David the most at times like these. He was the big brother, the one who could explain to his younger brothers why parents who said they loved each other couldn't get along.

Sailors in crisp, white uniforms held their wives' hands while strolling into the century-old Japanese building now converted into a chapel. Inside the church doors, aromas of burning candles and wood polish wafted through the sanctuary. A chandelier hung from the vaulted ceiling, and colorful flowers in vases lined the altar. The cross of Jesus hung behind the pulpit. While the organist played, an elderly Japanese man smiled and swayed while singing in the choir.

I walked down the aisle with the boys following me. Ryyan spotted one of his friends and went to sit with him. Laughlin darted behind him.

When the sermon began, the chaplain's voice faded away when my eyes fell on the sailor in front of me. His arm draped across his wife's shoulders, while a child fidgeted next to them. I glimpsed the empty space beside me. God, if marriage comes from you, why am I unhappy?

At the end of the church service, with my head bowed, tears fell on my lap. From behind me, a soft hand squeezed my shoulder. I quickly wiped my eyes and looked up. It was Ms. Phipps.

In the lobby, Ryyan introduced me to his friend, Joe, and his parents. They invited us to Sunday school. I accepted, remembering how I loved listening to stories about Jesus as a little girl in Sunday school.

With the boys in their classes, we went to the adult Sunday school. The teacher welcomed me with a big hug and introduced me to the class. She began class by praying for our service men and women in Iraq. During Sunday school, my unhappy marriage didn't feel so heavy while I was reading and studying the Bible.

After settling into school, our new home, and purchasing cell phones, Mark and I often explored the neighborhood. We window shopped at novelty shops which formed a border between the neighborhood and the city. People licking ice cream, strolling out of convenience stores, made Laughlin beg us to go inside. With cones in hand, we'd walk to the park. Sitting on a bench under cherry trees, we'd talk, watching Laughlin play with the Akimoto girls and other neighborhood children.

One conversation took us back to when we first moved to Georgia. Mark had inherited land on the family farm near a small town in Georgia. Abandoned stores downtown were the remains of a once-booming, agricultural town. Now deer hunters and logging supported the local economy. The nearest military base was two hours away. WWI and II monuments erected in the town square were as close to the military as residents wanted to get.

The white two-story Victorian we built sat on a knoll surrounded by woods thick with towering pine trees. A wrap-around porch, with high backed rocking chairs, hanging ferns, and flowering potted plants, provided cooling relief from the sweltering sun. Barns gray from the sun spotted the farm. Fresh cut hay, rolled up like fluffy blankets, sat on rolling hills. Mark fenced in thirty acres, cleared land for gardens, and purchased a bull and cows. Traveling in the military, we held onto our dreams of living in the country one day.

Now, watching Laughlin play, we didn't talk about our broken marriage. Only happy times. One evening, we received a phone call from David. He told us his unit would return to the US after Christmas. I cried, but this time, happy tears.

After a long day at school, and traffic on the drive home, I pulled into our driveway. Getting out the car, I heard a scale sounding from the piano inside Mewa's house, when a car pulled up. Mewa opened the door—a young boy scurried out to the car.

"Hello," Mewa said from her doorway. "How was school day?"

"Good. I'm tired, and have to cook dinner."

"Hard on wife," Mewa said. "Why not stay home?"

"I enjoy teaching," I said, taking a couple of grocery bags from the car. "Most American women work outside the home and take care of children, husbands and cook dinner."

"I stay home and give music lessons. Help family."

"Yes—kind of like your music lessons," I said.

"Let's shop Saturday?" she said.

I thought about the nice stores I'd seen in town. I'd only looked in the windows. This would give me the opportunity to shop inside.

Saturday morning, Mewa and I traipsed through the neighborhood. At the gravel parking lot, she pointed out a building where Japanese men gathered to socialize and drink sake. Passing the middle school, we stepped into the busy city.

We merged into shoppers crowding the sidewalks. Mewa stopped at a narrow entryway and pointed to a sign over the door written in Kanji. "Dishes," she said. Inside, cabinets and shelves were lined with crystal and china. I studied the unique designs. The work of a craftsman.

"You like," Mewa said.

"Beautiful," I said, admiring a crystal angel.

"Expensive," she said.

Stepping into the next shop, I saw the shelves were stocked with everyday household items I could afford.

For lunch, Mewa recommended a restaurant located near the train station. She helped me order a meal from the local cuisine. Savoring our food, we chatted about our families, how we needed to leave the children at home with their fathers more often, and laughed at a fat cat.

Bowing low, I thanked Mewa for lunch and the shopping trip.

"We do again soon," she said, bowing.

Early one morning, a cool breeze from the balcony nudged me out of the bed to get an extra blanket from the hall closet. Passing Ryyan's room, I saw his comforter crumpled next to an empty bed. I checked downstairs—the house was dark.

I put on my shoes and a coat over my pajamas. I rushed outside to the storage shed where Ryyan kept his bike. The shed was empty. I called Ryyan's cell phone and got the recording. I left a message.

I thought about waking Mark to help, but I knew where to look for Ryyan more than Mark did.

Driving toward Atsugi Base, where most of Ryyan's friends lived, I searched under the canopy of street lights.

Halfway there, I crossed the railroad tracks and saw Ryyan pushing his bicycle. I swerved into the right lane pulling up beside him.

"Where have you been? Do you know it's dangerous to ride a bicycle at night?" I said looking at him and trying to watch the road too.

"Hanging out with friends in Tokyo," he said, pushing his bicycle, not looking at me.

"Tokyo? What friends stay out this late?"

"I rode my bike to the train station to meet them, and we caught the train. That's what teenagers do in Japan."

"Why didn't you tell me you wanted to go?"

"You wouldn't have listened. You're too busy sightseeing and making friends."

His words tore pieces from my heart. I did miss our time together talking in the car on the way home from school, and I didn't really know who his new friends were except Joe from church.

"Will you please put your bike in the car?"

"I'll walk," he said.

I drove slowly behind Ryyan until he reached our drive way. He put his bike in the shed and entered the house. I shuddered in the cool morning air, hearing Ryyan's words ... too busy. While I was enjoying my new life, he was fighting for his independence as a teenager.

The next day, when Mark and I discussed Ryyan's early morning bicycle trip, I didn't share what Ryyan said about me. We wrote a contract with him including a curfew, traveling limitations, and requiring him to check messages on his cell phone.

CHAPTER 13—THE PEARL LADY

I loved our Japanese neighborhood even with all the inconveniences and extra work. I shopped for groceries more often because of our small refrigerator and cooked most evenings. Although American fast-food restaurants were nearby, I agreed with the guys—Japanese KFC just didn't taste like back home.

Our Japanese washer and dryer couldn't handle laundry for an American family. I found the laundromat on base with American brand washers and dryers. Once a week, I'd gather our laundry and drive to the base's laundromat. There I met interesting people from around the world and heard great stories.

On Saturday mornings, I'd stroll around the neighborhood alone, adoring the beautiful homes, flower gardens, and park. I wished Mark enjoyed living in Japan too. We'd never have to leave.

With the many families living in our cul-de-sac, you'd think noise complaints would be high. Yet, evenings were quiet, except when Mewa would grace us with her classical piano music.

The first quarter had ended and student progress reports were due. Mark, Doug, and I spent a couple of late evenings at school collaborating on comments for each student, and planned next semester's lessons. Doug and I gave Mark high fives. He survived the first quarter as an elementary school teacher.

Aromas of buttery popcorn and super cheesy nachos wafted through the night air under the bright stadium lights, where we were sitting in the stands. Cheerleaders flipping and tumbling across the sidelines waving pom-poms roused the fans. We had arrived safely at Ryyan's football game.

Ryyan spotted us in the bleachers, waved, flashed a big smile, and sprinted onto the field. When the referee yelled "touchdown," fans shot to their feet, clanging cow bells, and waving the Trojan flag. Sitting in the bleachers, cheering on the Zama Trojans—miles away from home—Friday night football in Japan.

For Thanksgiving, we attended the base commander's annual Thanksgiving dinner for the sailors and base employees in the sailors' dining hall—on the buffet table, loaded, steaming trays of ham, turkey, dressing, gravy, and sweet potato soufflé.

Going through two serving lines, the guys piled their plates high and found a table with a group of young sailors. Mark and Ryyan joined their conversation centered on Thanksgiving football and home.

On the wall, a wide screen monitor beamed in service members from Iraq, waving and blowing kisses as they told family members how much they missed them. Thinking about David eating Thanksgiving dinner in a war zone, I picked over dinner. I turned my attention to the young men—grateful we could share Thanksgiving Day with them.

With Christmas in two weeks, I got David's Christmas box mailed on time. Inside, I packed a miniature Christmas tree with tiny ornaments attached. I purchased his favorite television shows on video, and stuffed a stocking with his favorite snacks. Mark and the boys wrote David a special Christmas message. I placed mine on top.

Standing in line at the post office, I envisioned David opening the box in his tent and placing the tree in a corner for all the soldiers to admire. He would share his snacks while they laughed at videos. Christmas night, he'd read our letters, smiling thinking of us.

In Georgia, we'd visit a tree farm to select our Christmas tree. Mark said we had woods overflowing with trees in our backyard. We did, but I wanted a cedar. The tree's sweet aroma lingered in our home long past the Christmas season.

While we hunted for the perfect tree, the boys played among the acres of trees. Mark coaxed me along, insisting every tree was perfect. By the time I made a selection, a white moon had replaced the sun. Mark, waving a flashlight, chased the boys back to the truck.

This year, I shopped for a Christmas tree alone. I shopped at the base exchange, where I found decorations and live trees in the garden section. No cedars, but plenty of firs.

"What Japanese forest did these trees come from?" I said to the store clerk, pointing at the fir I'd chosen.

"Tree not from Japan. Seattle, Washington," he said, wrapping the tree in a net and hoisting it onto his shoulder. He leaned the tree next to my car. Motioning me to wait, he left, returning with a rope. He hoisted the tree onto the car's roof and tied it down. He stood back and announced, "The rope will hold."

Driving home, I received curious glances from Japanese drivers. As nature lovers, they probably wondered why I had a tree on top of my car.

Mark quickly set up the tree in the family room, releasing the scent of forest throughout our home. Once we'd added lights and ornaments, the tree packed an already crowded room. Mark and I both loved Christmas. We always gave each other cards. With property taxes due, and tuition for college classes, we spent our gift money on the boys.

We stayed up late on Christmas Eve wrapping gifts and eating cookies we'd baked for Santa. The next morning, we held each other while watching the boys' faces as they opened their gifts. One Christmas, we woke up to an unexpected snowfall. Our woods became a winter wonderland.

Christmas had come to our cul-de-sac with the lighted wreath on the door and our decorated tree visible from the window. Later in the evening, through the window, Mewa and her daughters faces glowed, fascinated by the twinkling white lights strung around the tree. I joined them outside.

"The birth of Jesus Christ," Mewa said.

"Yes," I said, impressed and embarrassed because she knew more about my culture than I did hers.

Christmas day was like every day in Japan—with people

shopping and commuting to work. Yet, I found joy despite our location. We sat in our decorated home, eating a dinner cooked in our American oven and laughing about last Christmas, when the boys chased a flock of turkeys through the woods. My family hadn't experienced this abundance of happiness in a long time. Although I missed David, Mom, and Pops, I saw a glimmer of hope for my broken marriage.

After dinner, David called. He thanked us for his Christmas gifts and said he missed home. With the need for additional soldiers to fight the war, David said his unit had been extended six months in Iraq. The joy of Christmas left me.

"You do know how to catch the train to Tokyo?" asked the school secretary, handing me a reservation for the New Sanno Hotel.

With Christmas break over, Ms. Phipps had scheduled me to attend a teachers' writing workshop in Tokyo. I'd not traveled in Japan alone, but with a driver, I'd agreed. Now, the driver had canceled.

I pulled out the Tokyo train map Doug had given me. Each stop had the city's name. With only a few passengers on board, I easily found a seat. The train flashed by narrow city streets congested with traffic and pedestrians. Wheels screeched as the train slowed to a stop.

Throngs of people pushed onto the train. With no empty seats available, people stood should to shoulder in the aisles. Pinned into my seat, with bodies blocking my view, I couldn't see the city's names on the station wall. The train pulled off. I touched the cell phone in my purse, but remembered talking on cell phones is forbidden on Japanese trains.

I was the only American on the train, and I was lost. As towns flew by outside the train's window, tears welled up. The stress of moving, starting a new job, David in Iraq, and a troubled marriage closed in on me like the people on the train.

"May I help you?" said a soft voice in English. A young Japanese girl dressed in a blue blazer and pleated skirt smiled down at me.

"Yes," I said, quickly. "I'm going to the New Sanno in Tokyo, and I'm afraid I missed my stop."

"I'm going to Tokyo. I'll show you the exit," she said. When the train stopped, she motioned for me to follow. I kept my eyes on her blue blazer as she wove through waves of people and passed through electronic gates. She stopped at a flight of stairs ascending toward an exit sign above a narrow door.

"At the top, make a left, walk two blocks and you will come to your hotel," she said.

Grateful, I bowed low, but when I rose, she'd disappeared into the sea of people. Looking at my watch, I exhaled. I would arrive at the workshop on time.

I wove my way around people on the sidewalks. No expensive showrooms lined this part of the city—only tall brick buildings, squeezed together, shooting up into the sky. On the sidewalk ahead, a group of Americans poured off a tour bus and entered the breezeway of a brick building with The New Sanno engraved over the entrance in fancy letters.

I followed the group through a security checkpoint out into a brick courtyard. Large, round ceramic pots bursting with countless hues of green plants surrounded the brick courtyard. Inside the hotel, crystal chandeliers hung from the vaulted ceiling, and cozy sitting areas with overstuffed love seats surrounded a stone fireplace with burning logs.

A sign with the Department of Defense Dependents Schools Teachers' Workshop directed me to a table where two ladies sat signing in teachers. They handed me a packet for the weekend, along with a room key.

Inside a large room filled with teachers, I found my name at a table. Waiters poured tea and served lunch, while we introduced ourselves. We chatted about traveling throughout the world to teach service members' children, this much-needed break, and attending the workshop in Tokyo.

After lunch, the workshop leader gave us our assignments for the day. We received a scoring rubric to evaluate students' essays. We went through examples and worked throughout the day taking short breaks. When we finished, the ladies invited me to dinner. Tempted, I declined. I'd had a long day.

Upstairs in my room, I called Mark. The boys had eaten dinner and were finishing homework. Mark had a lot of experience taking care of the children. Traveling with me in the military, he became one of the first Mr. Moms. He cooked, cleaned, checked homework, and kept the boys on their routine while I was away. When we left the military and moved back to the farm, Mark passed the reins to me. I went from full-time soldier to full-time mom and teacher. After we hung up the phone, I wanted to call Mark back. We hadn't slept apart from each other since I'd left the military. Would I miss him if we divorced?

After a long, hot shower and pajamas on, I lay in bed, relaxing and thinking of tomorrow morning. No sleepy children to wake up and get ready for school. No waiting in traffic. I opened a novel I've wanted to read for months. My eyelids were heavy—I didn't finish the first page.

A stack of student essays sat in the middle of our table after breakfast. As we worked through them, more essays arrived. At last, with our pile low, we took a break. In the lobby, Len, a lady from my group, waved me over to where she sat next to the fireplace.

"You mentioned at the table your son is in Iraq," she said, her face reflecting the concern of a close friend. "You must worry about him."

"Yes," I said, eyes burning.

"My son died in an automobile accident his freshman year of college. My marriage suffered, and we both wanted a divorce, but we decided to try again. Going to church together saved our marriage."

"What if your husband won't go?" I said.

"Keep praying for him. Don't nag or make him feel guilty. Pray your husband seeks God's will in his life. Wait and watch God transform him and soften his heart toward you." A smile lit her face.

Could I smile like Len if I lost David in Iraq, and have the courage to tell someone about my loss? Would my faith in God grow or falter enduring that kind of pain? Would my already fragile marriage fall apart? I wanted a faith like Len's. With people milling all around us, Len did something I didn't expect. Covering my hands with hers, she prayed aloud for David and my marriage. When she finished, her prayers had lifted a huge burden from my heart.

We finished grading essays before noon. Our workshop director said since we had completed our work, we could use the rest of our day sightseeing in Tokyo.

Len said, "Let's visit the Pearl Lady."

A cheer rose from the table.

"We visit her every year when we come to the workshop," she said. "The Peal Lady is expecting us."

We rode to the Roppongi district, a well-known, expensive shopping area, in a taxi and were dropped off at a towering brick building. An outside elevator went to the top floor and opened into a room the size of a hotel lobby.

Large framed photographs of celebrities wearing pearls hung on the walls. Former First Lady Barbara Bush, wearing her signature string of pearls, smiled wide from one photo. From another, Jackie Joyner-Kersee beamed as her husband draped pearls around her neck.

A Japanese lady in a stylish pantsuit, with silver streaks highlighting her short black hair, sat at a booth helping a couple in the back of the shop. Seeing us, she spoke to the couple briefly, then hurried over and embraced Len.

"Welcome to Wally's," she said, flashing a welcoming smile. "I'm the Pearl Lady. Look around while I finish with my customers."

We strolled around the shop browsing, with an assistant helping us try on the bracelets, earrings, and necklaces displayed on round, cherrywood tables throughout the store. The Pearl Lady waved us over to a glass display table and seated us in a booth. She disappeared behind a black satin curtain.

"She keeps the expensive pearls back there," Len said.

The Pearl Lady returned carrying a small, white rectangular box. Facing us, she opened it. We all took a deep breath and leaned forward. Inside lay a strand of creamy pearls with a pearl pendant designed in the shape of a sea shell.

"The pearls are from the Japanese sea. The necklace handcrafted especially for my DoDDS teachers," she said.

"Beautiful," I said.

"How much?" we said. The Pearl Lady wrote the price down. Our eyes widened.

"But for my dedicated DoDDS teachers, I have a special discount price," she said, quickly writing down another number.

" I like that price," Len said.

I shook my head at the new price and whispered to one of the teachers, "How can you afford this?"

"We save all year," she said with a smile and opened her purse.

I slid out of the booth and selected a bracelet from one of the round tables. The assistant wrapped my purchase while I waited for my group.

Back at the hotel, I thanked Len and the other teachers for the shopping trip and introducing me to the Pearl Lady.

I had a message waiting at the desk. A driver would take me home in the morning—good news to end a great trip.

When the driver dropped me off, a note sprawled in Mark's handwriting was taped to the door. Ryyan fell off his bicycle. Taken to Japanese hospital by ambulance. We're going to the hospital.

I called Mark's cell phone. No answer. I pressed my temples trying to figure out what to do next. I'd drive if I could find the hospital. About to go next door to ask Mewa for help, I heard the car door slam, and Laughlin bolted inside.

"Ryyan got to ride in the ambulance," he said.

Ryyan limped inside, with a bandage covering one eye and purple and black bruises on his face.

"What happened?" I said, holding back the scream rising in my throat.

"I'm okay," Ryyan said. "On my way to football practice, I lost control of my bike on the hill toward Zama Base. The guards on the gate saw me fall and called an ambulance. I practiced my Japanese talking to the EMTs. Doc says I'll heal fast. But my bike's busted up."

I examined Ryyan's bruised and bandaged face. He didn't own a bicycle in Georgia. I would never allow him to ride on a dangerous road. Tears streamed down my face, both because he was okay and because of the burden of guilt covering me whenever anything went wrong.

"Everything's okay, Mom. Ryyan won't ride his bike anymore," Laughlin said.

"Ryyan's fine, and the doctor says his face will heal quickly," Mark said, gently touching my shoulder.

Laughlin's arms squeezed my waist, and Ryyan's arm went around my shoulders. I hugged them both. I thought of Len and her son. I couldn't lose mine. Not on a bicycle. Not in a war.

CHAPTER 14—LIBERTY LANE

For two weeks, I'd worked late after school completing a project. Finished, I looked forward to Mark and I resuming our walks to the park.

"Ready to go?" I said, tying my shoes at the doorway.

"No," he mumbled, studying our hometown news on the internet.

"Come on, Mommy, let's go," Laughlin said, pulling me toward the door. Laughlin ran to play with the neighbor children—his curly brown hair sticking out like caramel popcorn against the Japanese children's straight black hair.

I sat on the park bench—alone. This was the third time I'd asked Mark to walk with us to the park—and he'd refused again. He'd also stopped going with us to the Japanese restaurants in our neighborhood, and had missed several after-school functions to come straight home. Was the dark cloud of neglect in my marriage, which I'd tried to escape, returning?

The next day at school, the sight of Mt. Fuji's snow-capped peak and the cool breeze made me zip my jacket on the way to Tony's classroom.

"Mark's isolating himself," I said. "He stays home all the time."

"I've seen this before," Tony said. "Mark's homesick. He needs to live near other Americans. The only way to help him is to move back on Atsugi Base."

"Return to the base? I love living in our home, our neighbors, and the park," I said.

"Sometimes you have to give up something you love in order to get what you want."

I called Yolanda. She agreed with Tony.

A few days later, I dropped by the housing office on base.

"Do you have an apartment available for a family of four?" I said to the housing officer.

"Yes," he said. "A garden apartment. You can take the keys and have a look."

I drove the short distance into a neighborhood with wide streets and freshly cut yards. I parked at a two-story, tan stucco duplex. A brick set of stairs led to a concrete landing in front of the apartment. I opened the door to a family room half the size of the one in our Japanese home. No foyer to take off your shoes. You didn't have to worry about scuffing up the dark square tile floors.

Floor-to-ceiling vertical blinds concealed a sliding glass door in the family room. I checked out the two bedrooms, bathroom, and kitchen. This place is smaller than our Japanese house.

I took two steps from the family room into the kitchen where American-sized appliances cut the small kitchen in half. Back in the family room, I opened the blinds. A bright Japanese sun burst into the dark room. A forest of leafy ferns, bamboos, and trees bordered the backyard and provided shade for a patio large enough for two chairs and a grill. I stood in the middle of the room and thought about what Tony had said. You have to give up something. God, help me make the right decision for my family.

Mark and Ryyan were both shocked when I showed them the apartment. They'd never thought I would consider moving back on base. They agreed the apartment was small, but the convenience of living on base made up for its size. Laughlin didn't have an opinion, he romped on the playground.

Mr. Dodson said he understood. Mark wasn't the first American to get homesick. I told Mewa we were moving.

She placed her hand over her heart and said, "Husband heart sick."

I nodded and gave her a long hug, promising to visit soon.

We nicknamed our new neighborhood Mayberry. The welcoming committee brought us dinner our first evening in the apartment. Later, Laughlin went to the playground and Ryyan visited friends. Mark and I explored the forest behind our apartment and found a walking path. That night, while I lay in bed, the grasshoppers called to each other in the forest. I closed my eyes, missing Mewa's evening concerts.

Mark's mood drastically improved when we move back on base. We additionally benefitted by eliminating the forty-minute drive each day, maneuvering through traffic and pedestrians. Living on base also placed us a few minutes from the Chapel of the Good Shepherd.

Our first Sunday on base, I invited Mark to church. He declined, saying he had papers to grade.

While we waited for church to start, an elderly Japanese man shuffled toward me with a big smile. I recognized him from the church choir.

"Hello, I'm Bearson," he said, placing a white origami crane in my hand. "You are sensei? Teacher?"

"Yes," I said, studying the perfectly folded edges of the cranes wings.

"You have husband?"

"Yes," I said my sadness, like water in a flood, rising.

"He will bring you happiness, like crane," Bearson said. "One day, I teach your students origami at American school."

"Sure," I said, forcing a smile.

He bowed low and walked away.

Inside the church's bulletin was an announcement for a marriage retreat at the New Sanno Hotel. We'd never attended one before. Persuading Mark to go, when he didn't come to church, felt impossible. Sitting in the pew, I asked God to draw Mark closer to him, and to give me patience to wait. When I arrived home, I taped the bulletin onto the refrigerator.

After a couple of months living on base, Laughlin's classmate Andrew invited him over to play. Laughlin begged to walk alone to Andrew's house. I was apprehensive, but Mark said to let him go—

he was growing up. Before Laughlin left, I gave him the stranger test.

"If someone asks you your name on the way to Andrew's house, what will you do?" I said.

"I'll tell them," Laughlin said, his innocent smile wide, exposing a pink gap where two front teeth were missing.

I cringed, wishing I could cancel his outing.

"No one's gonna hurt me, Mommy, because I love everybody, and everybody loves me," he said.

Laughlin was right—at least on Atsugi Base. Everyone he met on the base either worked with us or attended the chapel. I opened the door, kneeled looking into Laughlin's eyes, "If someone talks to you, please keep walking to Andrew's house," I said, hugging him tight.

I peeked out the window. Laughlin skipped down the sidewalk. I quickly phoned Andrew's mom and told her about our conversation. "Please call me when he walks through your door," I said.

One evening as Ryyan helped me carry groceries into the apartment, he pointed out a teenage boy dressed in black jeans and black T-shirt, his black hair shaved around the sides, the top spiked. Two studded black earrings pierced his ears. He walked along the sidewalk with his hands shoved into his pockets.

"Nobody wants to be his friend," Ryyan said.

"Why?" I said.

"Because he gets into trouble."

"Oh," I said, my heart softening toward the teenager. Young and already labeled a trouble maker.

With spring weather came baseball. Living on base, I enrolled Laughlin in baseball at the Atsugi Recreational Center. Mark volunteered to take him to practices, saying he'd have the opportunity to mingle with our students and their parents outside the classroom. Giving up something to get something was working.

CHAPTER 15—190 DAYS OF SCHOOL

"You're home early from school," I said to Ryyan.

"I skipped lifting weights. I have a DNA model to make for a chemistry project due tomorrow." he said, pulling a planner from his bookbag.

"I know your teacher didn't just give you this assignment."

He shrugged. "I need Styrofoam balls, craft sticks, and straws," he said, reading from his planner.

"And where are we supposed to get those materials?" I said, my last-minute-mom thermometer rising quickly. I called Yolanda for help. She suggested we catch the train to Yamoto, where a huge arts and crafts store was located down the street from the train station. From the Atsugi station, we were to get off at the first stop.

Entering the station, upset with Ryyan, I forgot my nervousness about riding the train. I followed Yolanda's directions and in fifteen minutes, the train wheels squelched to a halt in Yamoto. A half mile from the station, we entered a three-storied department store jam-packed with everything an arts and crafts lover could want.

"I'm sorry I blew up," I said on the platform, waiting on the train back to Atsugi City, with Ryyan's book bag full of supplies.

"I did wait until the last minute," he admitted. "Mom, do you know which train to take back home? You always have Ms. Yolanda with you when you ride the train. I think you're going the wrong way."

"Well, you have a choice. You can follow me or catch the train going in the opposite direction." I said.

A train rush up and the doors swung open. I hopped on. Ryyan quickly scanned the platform, hesitated, then jumped on behind me. Walking home from the Zama train station, I gave Ryyan a wink of confidence. He was the typical teenager—smarter than their old-fashioned parents.

The third nine weeks ended. Mark and I were off to a great start. We'd both received good evaluations from Ms. Phipps, although during one of her observations in my class, a F-18 roared over while I taught a lesson.

Ms. Phipps said, "Mrs. Smith, you must count to ten whenever a jet flies over the school. I couldn't hear a word you said."

Embarrassed, I gave the lesson again.

Teaching with DoDDS was a dream job. I seldom had disciplinary problems, and students were eager to learn. If classwork or behavior became unsatisfactory, their mom or dad was notified and areas of concern, promptly corrected.

In the classroom, I understood the stress of frequent moves and separation from parents and family back home. My heart broke when a child cried during class or refused to complete an assignment because their parent was out to sea. I had once been that child.

Offering classes in both Japanese culture and language, Lanham embraced the Japanese customs and traditions. We gaped at Japanese women pounding rice with heavy wooden mallets in a large mortar into sweet, smooth, sticky mounds. Japanese dancers charmed us with their daring acrobatics and graceful movements across the gym floor, and we stomped our feet to the rhythm of Yamato drummers.

Some days, from my classroom window, I'd watch Mark crossing the Red Top, with children laughing and playing behind him, like the Pied Piper. When the students came to my class, they'd asked if Mark's "Boy Wilson" stories were true—stories of his childhood in the country—and if he'd caught a twenty-pound fish in the pond.

For a military child like me, the idea of country life and growing up with the same friends from kindergarten through twelfth grade was unimaginable. I too was drawn to Mark's stable home life and the colorful characters he knew well.

Ryyan did well his first year in high school. He received an award at the sports banquet for Most Improved Defensive Player, and we were proud parents when he made honor roll. One evening, Mark and I noticed a two-door sedan speed up to the apartment and drop Ryyan off. The driver was the teenager dressed in black we'd seen walking down the sidewalk when we first moved into the neighborhood.

"Who's that?" Mark said.

"One of Ryyan's friends from school," I said.

"Have you met him?"

"Not really. His dad's in the Navy."

"We might need to speak to Ryyan about his friend driving fast in a neighborhood."

I didn't tell Mark Ryyan's friend had a reputation for getting into trouble.

Before summer break, teachers chatted with excitement about their plans for the summer. Many of the single teachers were going to Europe. Yolanda gave English lessons to Japanese children after school. She would stay in Atsugi City to continue their lessons and later, fly to California. Doug traveled to DC every summer to visit family and friends. Tony and his family would travel in Japan.

David wouldn't return from Iraq until the middle of the summer. I wanted to stay in Japan a couple of weeks. When I got the nerve to ask Mark, it was too late. He'd already packed his suitcases for home. I dreaded returning to Georgia and the flood of bad memories waiting for me—I wished the summer was already over.

CHAPTER 16—HOMECOMING SOUTHERN STYLE

Mark raced the rental van from Atlanta to our farm and pulled into the driveway before the orange sun set below the woods behind our house. Hopping out of the van, Mark and the boys dashed toward the house. I loitered behind, gawking at our home as though I'd never seen it before. Laughlin's popped his head outside the garage door.

"Mommy, come inside," he shouted. "There's food on the table, and the house smells good."

From the kitchen, mingled aromas of spaghetti sauce and garlic bread wafted through the house. A covered dish sat on the table. I peeled back the foil. A spaghetti casserole oozed with yellow cheese. A pitcher of sweet tea and garlic bread in a basket sat on either side. A note, resting against the casserole, read, Welcome home Smith family. Sam and Mary.

After dinner, Mark stepped outside into the summer night. A light popped on in the barn. Ryyan was stretched out on the bed in David's room. He begged to use it until David returned. Laughlin lay sleeping on the floor with toys scattered around him. I picked him up and put him in bed. My heart torn, I watched him sleep. No scary cat around to peer into his room—only a full moon, shining on stuffed animals in the window sill, and a warm summer breeze.

The next morning, I sat on the porch, watching Mark toss weeds and dead plants from the garden. As a third-generation farmer, Mark loved the soil he was raised on. With summer break, and plenty of sun and rain, Mark planted large gardens with the tractor his father left him. He plowed up the soil and planted purple hull peas, silver queen corn, butter beans, and everyone's favorite, watermelon.

In the smaller garden, Mark showed the boys and me how to plant tomatoes, cucumbers, and squash. Harvesting required bending over in the hot sun picking vegetables, but the family had fun working together.

Mom arrived to pick up Laughlin. He'd visit a few weeks with her and Pops before David returned. Ryyan spent time catching up with friends. One evening, he nagged me about getting a driver's license. He said his friends had theirs—and jobs.

I made a deal with him. He could get his learner's permit this summer, and when we got back to Japan, I'd consider letting him get a driver's license and a job. His wide grin and tight hug said "okay."

While we waited for David to contact us, I planned the menu and decorations for our celebration. Mark cranked up his tractors, and complained there wasn't enough time to grow a garden. Instead, he'd prepare the ground for next summer, when we moved back to Georgia. He sat on the tractor and waited for me to confirm his plan. I didn't. He revved the tractor engine and sped off.

Our first Sunday home, I wanted to attend church, but with Laughlin at Mom's and Ryyan with friends, I stayed home—too embarrassed to sit in the pew alone.

We'd been home two weeks and hadn't heard from David. Every news station showed service members returning from Iraq into the arms of their loved ones. Although we have generations of veterans in our family, I didn't encourage David to join the army. I wanted him to attend college and experience life with other young people.

His senior year in high school, I arrived home from work one afternoon to find David, Mark, and an army recruiter sitting at the kitchen table.

"I know you want me to go to college, Mom, but I decided enlisting in the army will help me pay for college. When I get out, I'll enroll. You and Dad have to sign, giving your consent, because I'm not eighteen." He slid a piece of paper toward me.

I studied Mark's face. He looked away. The decision was made without me.

The next school year, I was in charge of our school's first fund raiser. Needing last minute items, I left school on my break and shopped at our local grocery store. Inside the store, a gasp rose from the shoppers viewing the TV screen.

"That's not an accident," someone shouted. "A second plane hit the towers."

I watched in horror the billowing black smoke and crumbling towers. I raced back to school, comforted my students, and tried to make sense of what happened. A few months later, David called and said he was deploying to Iraq.

Now, desperate to know if David had arrived safely from Iraq, I called the First Armored Division in Germany. They assured me the soldiers would contact their families when their plane landed. Right now, their location was classified.

I stood in David's bedroom looking at his senior prom picture on the desk, football trophies lined up on the book shelf. His favorite music groups' posters were tacked on the wall. Ryyan burst into the room with a phone in his hand.

"Someone wants to speak with you," he said.

"Mom," David said, "I'm safe in Germany and catching the next flight to Georgia."

While I spoke with Mom and Pops giving them the good news, tears of joy overflowed. Mom said, "Thank you, Jesus."

On the day of David's arrival, I busied myself preparing for his welcome home party. Fresh ferns hung beneath the wrap-around porch rafters, and zinnias grew wild in flower pots on the front lawn. I replaced the faded yellow ribbons on the porch with new ones. The American flag rested in its holder waving over a freshly cut lawn. Red, white, and blue balloons floated in the air from the porch railings. When Mom and Laughlin arrived, he made sure we didn't forget the balloons for the mailbox at the road.

Mark and Ryyan left early to pick up David from the airport. Sam brought Sonny Boy over and placed him in his pen. We didn't want him to miss David's homecoming. While I prepared food, my eyes grew tired watching for our SUV through the kitchen window. Finally, our SUV eased up the gravel driveway.

My heart pounding, I ran outside and stopped on the front porch. David stepped out of the car grinning, his body thin and skin baked golden brown by the desert sun. Bounding up the steps, he flashed a dimpled smile and tied me up in a hug. "I missed you, Mom."

Breaking loose from me, he yelled, "Gma!"—sweeping her frail body into the air. She wobbled when he set her down. She had picked up the phone early mornings when he called from Iraq, comforting him with stories of God's love—like she did for Pops when he served in Vietnam.

When family and friends arrived, "Thank you for your service," and slaps on the back rang throughout the front porch and yard. While our guests sat at long tables in the front yard, Mom, Mary, and I served smoked barbecued ribs, fresh corn, peas from Sam's garden, Mom's potato salad, pound cake with strawberries, and pitchers of sweet tea.

After dinner, Laughlin took baby steps onto the porch, carrying a three-layer cake, with the "1" and "9" candles lit and stuck into a double-thick layer of chocolate icing. He set the cake in front of David to celebrate his nineteenth birthday. The birthday card and gift we mailed him from Japan to Iraq on his birthday were not enough. Everyone sang "Happy Birthday" while David wiped his eyes and blew out the candles.

Later in the evening, while a peach-colored sun sank beneath the pine thicket, the family gathered on the porch, settling back into rockers and spreading out on the steps to hear Mark's "Boy Wilson" tales. After everyone had gone home, Mark carried a sleeping Laughlin upstairs to bed. We left David and Ryyan in the family room playing video games.

Around two a.m., I checked on the boys, peeking into their rooms. Ryyan and Laughlin slept soundly. Ryyan's feet touched the footboard. He'd grown in Japan. I crept down the hallway to David's bedroom. The door was ajar. I eased inside, pulled the covers over his shoulders, and thanked God for bringing him home safely.

Back in our bedroom, the songs of night birds and warm light from the harvest moon bathed the room. Mark's strong hands moved softly over my body—the closeness and passion from our first years of marriage rushed back—from a time when love was spontaneous and required no thought. His heavy breathing excited and frightened me at the same time. But I pushed his hands away, turned over, and slid close to the bed's edge—a safe, familiar place. A place where I didn't have to pretend everything was all right. The cicadas chirping grew louder as I escaped into my own world of pain and unforgiveness.

The next morning, Mark cooked pancakes, stacking them high on a platter, drizzling them with cane syrup, while the boys sat around the table sharing stories about Iraq and Japan. After breakfast, we trekked through the cool woods with our cane poles and freshly dug worms. A narrow path under the wood's canopy opened into a tear-drop shaped pond where water lilies floated and cattails grew along the edge.

After a picnic lunch, the boys skipped rocks in the pond, while Mark caught all the fish. At the house, Mark cleaned fish, battered them in yellow corn meal, and dropped them into a pan of hot grease. Blue gill, brim, and bass served with coleslaw and crispy hush puppies loaded our plates. We washed our food down with sweet tea until only a pile of fish bones remained on the kitchen table.

A week before David returned to his unit in Germany, I gazed out the window while washing dishes. Mom's red roses bloomed on a trellis against the house. Darting through the air, a hummingbird hovering in midair—stole nectar from a trumpet flower. Arms circled me in a hug.

"That feels good." I said to David.

"Yeah, and the family together without you and Dad ..."

"You can say it. Arguing all the time."

I wish I could erase David's memory. He had to grow up too fast watching his parents yell at each other.

"How are things with you and Dad?" he said, picking up a dish to dry.

David knew I wanted to leave his Dad. During one argument, I hurled the word divorce at Mark. I turned to walk away and saw the boys standing inside the door staring at me.

"Japan has helped."

"Ryyan and Laughlin look happy."

"I stopped fighting with Dad in front of them. In fact, I don't fight with him at all anymore," I said.

"That's good, Mom, but you shouldn't hold your feelings inside."

"We have one more year. I'm not ready to come home."

"Does Dad know?" he said, turning to look at me.

"I think he does. We don't talk about it."

"Mom, do you think we can all go to church together tomorrow? In Iraq, thinking of our church helped me through some tough times."

"Of course, I'll go. You'll have to ask Dad."

Drying the last dish and moving back to look out the window, David said, "I missed flowers and birds in Iraq. Wars kill nature. That's what wars do ... they kill everything."

David hugged me again. "I love you, Mom."

"I love you more."

Sunday morning, in a country church tucked up against tall, thick pines, we all sat together on one pew. The choir belted out "What a friend we have in Jesus" as the pianist sat on the edge of her stool, swaying to the music, hands waving up and down through the air conducting the choir.

Our church attendance while I served in the military was sporadic with our many moves and my weekend duty. Growing up in the military, my family attended services on base. We sang from the hymnbook while the organ played and the chaplain taught from the Bible. Here the words from the songs were led by the older members, and the pastor's sermon, shouted from the pulpit, moved people to cry.

After church, David received another hero's welcome. The pastor called him to the altar for prayer. While David stood in front, the ushers lined up the congregation in the aisle. The men walked by laughing and shaking his hand. The women gave him big, warm hugs.

David tossed a football to Ryyan and Laughlin in the hay field, while I sat on the front porch swing. David leaves for Germany tomorrow. His unit would not return to Iraq. These past two weeks, I'd had my family back—the family I had when we'd first moved to the country. One overflowing with closeness, laughter, and love.

David's fresh haircut, sharp military uniform, and polished shoes drew attention inside the Atlanta International Airport. People stopped, shook his hand, and thanked him for his service.

After saying good-bye, Mark grabbed David and held onto him for a while. Ryyan and Laughlin slapped David's hand saying, "See ya." I gave David a quick hug and kiss. Walking toward the terminal, David turned around and waved. I forced a smile. Please God, help me hold it together for David.

Mark came near and squeezed my hand. "He'll be fine."

The next day, I washed clothes and packed suitcases, while Mark, once again, prepared the farm for our nine-month absence. The day before our return to Japan, Mark handed me a piece of paper.

"Read this," he said.

I skimmed over the paper—our teaching contract with the Department of Defense.

"We have one more year."

He walked away.

I didn't want to come back. We had spent more time together these past nine months than we had in years. Wounds we'd inflicted on each other still needed healing.

My Sunday school teacher had taught the class about prayer. Jesus said ask in my name and it will be given to you. I'm asking, Jesus. Give Mark and me a third year to grow closer to you and each other.

CHAPTER 17—TINA

When we returned to Japan, Ryyan quickly reminded me of our conversation about his driver's license. With a learner's permit from the US, he only needed a road test given on base to get his license.

I sighed with relief when I learned teenagers were not allowed to drive off base in Japan with a driver's license. Ryyan found a job at the food court. A huge grin settled on his face when he backed my car out the parking lot— his first day driving to work.

Our second school year as a team, Mark, Doug, and I planned a hike through the forest on base to start the school year. After school and on weekends, Mark mapped out a trail where students would encounter trees, flowers, bugs, and a stream.

Doug and I put together an activity sheet where students collected insects and plants, took water samples, and journaled about animals living in the forest's understory.

Following Mark's safety briefing, he led excited students and parents equipped with backpacks and lunches into the forest on a day with low heat and floating white clouds in a blue sky.

Stopping at a clearing, Mark gently hushed the children. He explained—in a way ten-year-olds could understand—the forest's ecosystem, how plants and animals are dependent on each other. While he had their attention, he told a quick story about how the notorious Boy Wilson chased him through the Georgia woods. With cheers and laughter the children were dismissed to explore the forest.

At lunch time, I sat with a group of children next to a stream while Mark and another group sat on the other side. Eating lunch and laughing with the children, I caught Mark smiling at me—a smile I'd seen before. When we first met. On our wedding day. Each time I told him we were having a baby. Maybe there was hope for us yet. I smiled back.

The beginning of the second semester, I checked the morning email. I had a new student, Tina, coming from a DoDDS school in Germany.

When the class filed in, she sat in back of the classroom. Not wanting to embarrass her, I walked to her desk, and asked her to share with the class her favorite places, hobbies, or anything she wanted us to know about her. She looked the class over and shook her head.

Having been the new student many times, I assured her in a few days, she'd have plenty of friends.

Back at my desk, I went over the class roll, while the students were reading.

"Mrs. Smith, she's bothering me," a student said.

I looked up. Everyone pointed to Tina. "She's making sounds, and I can't work," another student said.

Tina gave me an impish grin.

This seating arrangement isn't going to work.

"Tina, will you sit in a desk up front, please."

She grabbed her book bag and meandered to the front—tripping in a pretense of falling. The class burst out in a roar of laughter.

"Tina," I said, my voice rising. After twenty minutes of fun, the students settled down, leaving only a few minutes for class.

After another day of Tina's class interruptions, I needed to know how Mark handled her rambunctious behavior.

"How's the new student in your class?

"Fine, she's smart."

"What about her behavior?"

"No problem."

"Really. She disrupted most of my class period."

"What about Doug's class?" Mark said.

"He said Tina wasn't a problem."

"Have you thought about what you're doing to cause her to seek attention in class?"

"Really ... remember I'm the elementary teacher."

"Why don't you come to my room on your break and observe her."

The next day, I peeked through Mark's window. Tina sat at her desk, focused working on math problems Mark wrote on the board. No pencil throwing, yelling out, or walking around the classroom bothering other students.

"Okay, tell me what you're doing," I said.

"First, I'm not boring," he said.

Really?

"Just kidding," he said. "I teach math and science, and Doug teachers social studies. Maybe it's what you've selected for her to read."

"I give her a choice. We go to the library."

"Maybe she doesn't know what to choose. She likes math and science."

"May I keep Tina with me part of your class tomorrow?"

"Sure, I have another suggestion. Smile. The other students know you're not mean. Tina doesn't."

The next day, Tina and I went to the library. Along the way, she chattered about her last school, her best friend she'd left behind, and her siblings. I listened and smiled until my face hurt.

Sitting in the library, I asked Tina what kind of books she'd like to read. She shrugged her shoulders.

"Let's look through the stacks and see what we can find." I said.

We sat cross-legged on the carpet and selected three books from the science section. "Which one?" She chose a book on insects. We took turns reading, and she talked excitedly about each insect as we turned the book's pages.

As she closed the book, Tina asked if she could check it out and read it at home.

I waited on Tina to check out the book. This time, smiling didn't hurt.

The next day, during independent reading, Tina asked, with her insect book in her hand, to visit the library. Now, I had a peaceful classroom and most importantly, I had another student who loved to read.

Ryyan joined the wrestling team his sophomore year instead of playing football. He said they traveled more, and he liked the coach. Laughlin slowly grew out of playgrounds and spent too much time watching television. I suggested he join the youth basketball team. I wasn't the only parent with the idea. Most of Laughlin's playground buddies were on the team.

At school, during lunch, I'd bring leftovers from dinner, and Mark would join me in my classroom. One day, I rattled on about how carefree our lives were traveling in the military never having to stay anywhere for more than three years, and ...

"Stop talking," Mark said, he leaned in and kissed me.

"What's that for?"

"I wanted to know what kissing you during the day felt like."

I turn into a blushing bride all over again.

The boys and I continued to attend church and Sunday school. Going without Mark had become easier. I had made friends and liked my church family. Sunday school helped my prayer life and personal Bible study to grow. I'd learn to pray short prayers during the day, and left the class with questions. During my time alone, I eagerly sought answers in the Bible.

This year, we had Thanksgiving dinner in our apartment. I had met a single sailor in church from Georgia and invited him to dinner. With David in Germany this Thanksgiving, I wanted to share our home and dinner with a service member away from home. I called Mom for help, and cooked a Thanksgiving dinner with all the trimmings. The young sailor and my guys eating, and later, whooping and slapping each other watching the football game, made my heart swell.

CHAPTER 18—A CROWN OF GLORY

Mom's curly, white hair moved through a sea of passengers flowing through the Narita Airport in Tokyo. Over the summer, we'd made plans for her to visit at Christmas.

Mom, no stranger to airports, had traveled with Pops many times across the country, and this was her second international flight. Mom had visited us sixteen years ago in Germany for Ryyan birth. Pops stayed at home, saying he had had enough long flights to Asia during the Vietnam War.

Hurrying toward Mom, I became a little girl again, heart beating with joy at reuniting with her. I took Mom's luggage and navigated her through the airport into a shuttle van heading for Atsugi.

The driver dropped us off at the apartment. The guys met us at the door along with the smell of our live fir tree, decorated for Christmas, and spaghetti and garlic bread ready for dinner. After eating, Laughlin took Mom to several playgrounds in the neighborhood. After their walk, as she was ready to rest, I took her to the Atsugi Base Guest House. Impressed with her accommodations, a bedroom and bath, small family room, and full-size kitchen, she'd stay longer, she said, if Pops wouldn't get upset.

The next day, we attended Christmas Eve service. The Chapel of the Good Shepard's altar bloomed with red and white poinsettias, and along with the bells, the choir sounded like angels from heaven.

After service, I introduced Mom to Bearson. Smiling wide, he pointed to her white hair and said, "crown of glory." Mom pointed to his bald head and said, "wisdom." They sat together on a pew chatting like old friends.

Late that night, we got our phone call from Germany. David, safe and having a good time in Germany, had received his Christmas box.

On Christmas day, Mom and I cooked dinner. We used substitutions for her home cooking, but the guys said they couldn't tell the difference.

After dinner, we gave Mom her gifts first. She aahed over the handmade picture frame Laughlin gave her—with his picture inside. Ryyan presented her with perfume he'd purchased with the money he earned from working, and Mark and I gave her a crystal rose pin we'd purchased from the Navy Exchange. We all received hug and kisses.

Mom asked Laughlin to bring her suitcase. When she opened it, Laughlin opened his mouth in surprise, discovering the wrapped gifts inside. Mom gave Laughlin his gift. Of course, he received the video game he'd wanted. Mark and Ryyan unwrapped their gifts, finding their traditional sweaters and socks. I cut my eyes at them. They smiled and thanked her in unison for their gifts.

When Mom handed me a gift, I lifted it up and down to determine its weight. I slowly removed the gift wrapping. Tin foil covered the shape of a loaf pan. I sniffed the familiar fruity outside. Peeling back the foil, I shouted—Mom's homemade fruitcake. The guys frowned as I offered them a piece of heaven on Earth.

Yolanda helped me plan an itinerary of exciting places to take Mom where the train rides and car trips were short.

We gave Mom a tour of our classrooms. I let Mark and Mom talk alone while I waited in my classroom. She soon joined me there. Mom, impressed with our classrooms, said teaching didn't suit her. She didn't have the patience, and children were different from when she grew up.

Laughlin took her to the Red Top. While they sat on the swings, the clouds unveiled Mt. Fuji, showing off its majestic beauty.

We had lunch at the Food Court, ordering a meal from where Ryyan worked. Looking professional, he took Mom's order and money, cooked her hamburger and fries, and presented her meal, with soda, to her over the counter. The way Ryyan's chest popped out when Mom told everyone Ryyan was her grandson, you'd have thought he owned the restaurant.

When Ryyan's shift ended, we all took a trip to Zama Base. Ryyan pointed out his school to Mom as we drove toward the football field. Out on the field, she held her arms out wide and chuckled while he tossed her a football and made a fake tackle.

The day before Mom left, I took her back to the old neighborhood, showed her our first home, and we made a surprise visit to Mewa.

Mom and I took a short train ride to a fancy nail shop for a manicure in Ebina city.

"This place is expensive," she said.

"It's a late Christmas gift, Mom, and I'm getting a manicure too."

"Well, okay, it's nice to waste money on yourself sometimes," she said.

While we were eating lunch at a café, I admired Mom's emerald wedding ring, Pops's fiftieth anniversary gift to her. At nineteen, Mom married Pops. He lived down the street from her, and they'd grown up together. He'd already joined the military and was stationed at Fort Ord, California, when he proposed. He sent her a train ticket to California where, she said, Pops had made arrangements with a one-armed judge to marry them at the courthouse.

We all traveled with Pops to his many duty assignments. Although he grew up in the city, wherever we lived, he'd rent a cabin in the woods. If a pond, lake, or ocean, were nearby, we went fishing.

Mom and Pops were good parents teaching us to love God, family, and country. They had arguments, but always made up.

"How did you and Dad stay married this long?" I said.

"We almost didn't," she said.

"Really, why?"

"He stayed away from home a lot serving twice in Vietnam and working late hours in the military. When he came home, he went fishing."

I remembered happy times on our all-day fishing trips with Pops, while Mom stayed home.

"We also didn't have a lot of money. I found out one time he gambled his whole pay check. He later told me he won it back and had learned his lesson."

"Pops wasted money? He counts every penny."

"I got a job to help out. Your dad didn't like my working." Mom picked up her tea cup and sipped tea. "A job made things worse.

Now I had to cook, clean, and take care of four children. I was stubborn and wouldn't quit my job. I acted mad at him all the time. I'd cry late at night when you children went to sleep."

The crying part sounded like me.

"I spent some of my money and called my mom—cost me a whole paycheck. We didn't have cell phones. I complained to her about your dad and asked her to help me get back home with you kids. I waited for her to tell me where to pick up the tickets, but instead she asked me how much time I spent on my knees talking to God. I admitted very little. She told me to pray and ask God to help me stay married."

"Did things get better?"

"No, they got worse, but I got better. I prayed more for your dad and me, and I took you kids to church and Sunday school. Later, help came from everywhere. Your dad got a promotion and new duty assignment where he wasn't gone all the time, and I took up fishing," she said, tickled by the memory.

"Why are you just now telling me this?"

"You didn't need to know until now." Looking inside her teacup, she smiled and said, "This green tea wouldn't be so bad if you dumped sugar in it."

The night before Mom left, we all gathered at the guest house where we ate freshly baked homemade chocolate chip cookies and helped Mom pack. No one wanted to say goodbye.

The next morning, Mom and I got up early to catch the van back to the airport. Watching Mom's crown of glory disappear in the customs line, I could only hope to wear a crown like hers one day.

CHAPTER 19—A NEW HARLEY

The email from Ms. Phipps on Monday said teachers had two weeks to decide if they were returning to teach next year. A teaching contract was attached. I rushed to Yolanda's classroom after school.

"Did you see the email?" I said.

"Yes," she said, wiping off a student table. "I've decided to go back home and teach. Mickey needs more time with her dad."

I walked over to the table and squeezed her tight.

"I'll miss you," I said.

"We can keep in touch," she said, wiping her eyes.

"I've got two weeks to convince Mark to stay another year."

Yolanda stopped tidying up the room and looked at me.

"I didn't want to tell you, but since we've returned from summer break, Mark's been telling students and parents this is his last year teaching in Japan."

I took a deep breath, holding my anger in against Mark.

"I can't go back yet," I said. "I had a good summer—but because we spent time with David."

"Tell him how you feel."

She didn't understand. That's when we'd argue.

Smoky clouds covered Fuji as I walked across the Red Top. Yolanda was right. I needed to be honest with Mark. I picked up my students from the lunchroom. In our reading group, I tried to focus on the story and my students' voices while they read. But my mind kept going back and forth between the lessons and how to tell Mark I wanted to stay in Japan for another year. Maybe he didn't see the email. I'd have more time to convince him.

Back at the apartment, I prepared dinner while I waited for Mark and Laughlin to return from baseball practice.

"Hey, Mom," Laughlin said, hugging me with his baseball glove on.

"How's practice?"

"Coach said I'm the best pitcher on the team."

"I already know," I said, smiling down into a sweet face painted bronze by the sun. "Go start your homework while I finish dinner."

Laughlin disappeared into his room, and Mark walked into the kitchen.

"Did you see the email?" he said.

I opened a cabinet and pretended to search for an item. I turned to face Mark and took a deep breath.

"I think we need to talk about staying another year," I said.

"There's nothing to say. We both agreed. Two years."

"Will you please reconsider. I'm just getting use to living here and ..."

"Oh, no. You're not doing this to me. The job is great, but our time is up. If you won't go, I'm leaving and taking the boys." He turned and walked away. Moments later, the front door slammed.

I sat at the kitchen table. Now what was I going to do. Mark had never mentioned leaving me before. I was the one always threatening to get a divorce. And to take the children too?

"Mommy, is dinner ready? Where's Dad?" Laughlin said, coming back into the kitchen.

I rose quickly and walked over to the stove. "He's gone for a walk," I said with my back turned, holding back tears. "Here's dinner. Let's eat."

Ryyan soon joined us. I put Mark's plate in the oven. We tackled homework in a quiet house. Laughlin asked about Mark again. Ryyan gave me a sideways glance. He'd experienced the aftermath of our arguments before. I told Laughlin his dad had papers to grade at school.

The boys and I were in the bed when I heard the front door open and sounds from the television.

Mark and I avoided each other the rest of the week, briefly speaking about the boys and our students. Mark left campus each day for lunch without me. I packed my lunch and ate alone in my classroom. I'd lose if I stayed and Mark took the boys, and I'd lose if I went back to the farm. I remembered the Scripture from Sunday school to not worry and to pray.

One day, during silent reading time, one of my students came to my desk with red-rimmed eyes.

"What's wrong?" I said.

"My mom and dad are getting a divorce," he said. "Mom says my sister and I have to move away and leave my dad here. I don't know if I'll ever see him again."

Tears spilled from his eyes. I pulled him into my arms.

He was a good student—smart, helpful around the classroom, and well-liked by his classmates. What would happen to him and his sister? After school, I went to see the counselor.

"This happens a lot," she said. "Wives are tired of living on base with the children while their husbands are at sea. When some sailors do come home, they spend more time at bars than with their families. Children always get caught in the middle. Let's hope she changes her mind."

My heart sank the next day when my student didn't show up, and I received his transfer notice requesting his grades for the semester.

Throughout the week, my student's tearful words replayed in my mind. Would Laughlin become distraught if Mark left, taking him away from me? What about Ryyan? Worry set in as I went through the motions of teaching and being a mom for the next few days.

Thursday after school, I stood looking out the kitchen window. A couple strolled down the sidewalk, arms entwined like a Christmas bow. A child rode a bike with wobbly training wheels alongside them. Tears spilled over. I heard the door open and quickly wiped my face. I turned around, expecting Laughlin. Instead, Mark stood at the kitchen door.

"Where's Laughlin?" I said.

"He's at the playground with friends from school." Mark walked over to me. "Does staying mean that much to you?"

"Yes," I said the lump in my throat rising.

"I'll stay another year, but I want something."

My heart beat fast, waiting.

"I want a Harley, like the one at Yokota Base, and I want us to attend the marriage retreat," he said, taking the bulletin off the refrigerator door and handing it to me. "If I took the boys away, we couldn't make it without you."

I couldn't hold back the tears any longer—they flowed with love and joy. The next day, I told Yolanda the good news. She spilled over with happiness for me knowing how badly I wanted to stay, and recommended Mark teach her ESL students when she resigned. Friday, I handed the office assistant our newly-signed contracts, and thanked God for another year in Japan.

CHAPTER 20—HIROSHIMA

Yolanda suggested I take the family to Hiroshima to see the Peace Memorial Museum for Spring Break. She'd booked a trip there last year, through the tour agency on base. She and Mickey had a great time.

When Ryyan read the book Hiroshima for a class assignment. I'd picked up a copy and read along with him. After reading the book, we couldn't live in Japan and not visit Hiroshima. When I asked the guys if they wanted to go, the answer was a unanimous "yes." We were all ready to explore another part of Japan.

In a bus equipped with wide seats, TV screens, and a cooler loaded with complimentary snacks, we departed Wednesday evening, for the thirteen-hour, all-night bus ride to the southernmost part of Japan.

The bus pulled up to the entrance of the Grand Prince Hotel—a skyscraper hotel, built along the blue waters of the Seto Inland Sea. We checked into our rooms and freshened up before our first stop, the Peace Memorial Museum.

In Hiroshima, our bus crossed bridges with peaceful rivers flowing beneath them. Five rivers run throughout the city, giving it the name 'City of Water,' our guide told us. The city's tall buildings resembled Tokyo's, but the trees, rivers, and mountain range gave it the feel of a country town.

On the way to the Peace Memorial Museum, we passed the Hiroshima Castle. Our tour guide said the original castle had boasted a five-storied pagoda and a moat. The atomic bomb dropped on the city in 1945 destroyed the castle. The new one is a museum where visitors can examine artifacts from the bomb. A breathtaking view of the city and flowing rivers is visible from the top of the castle, she said.

As we crossed a bridge, a steel dome came into view, sitting atop a towering, steel building with its interior gutted out and huge rectangular openings where windows were once located. Our guide explained the Hiroshima Prefectural Industrial Hall had absorbed the powerful explosion and heat from the bomb and had burst into flames. The thick outer walls and the steel dome had escaped complete destruction because the impact of the blast had come from overhead.

Tragically, the people working inside the building died instantly. Fire completely gutted the building's interior. Now, referred to as the Atomic Bomb Dome, the skeleton frame stands silhouetted against the sky. A hush fell over the bus as we passed the Dome's grisly frame —showcasing the destructive power of nuclear weapons.

We exited the bus at the Peace Memorial Park and strolled up a wide concrete sidewalk lined with cherry trees and bordered by a green lawn. Walking through the park, we only heard the sounds of nature.

In the middle of the park stood the Memorial Cenotaph, an arch covering a tomb, the design representing a shelter for the atomic bomb victims' souls. Below the granite arch, a stone vault holds the names of people who died from the bomb.

Next, our guide directed us into the museum's lobby, where people quietly milled around. Even the children whispered out of respect for the victims and their families. Our guide handed out museum maps and gave us miniature brown boxes with headphones—audio guides to take us on the museum tour.

Mark and Ryyan explored upstairs, and Laughlin and I stayed on the main floor. We began the tour with a short video on the atomic bomb and a brief history of World War II.

Walking through the museum, we viewed collections of black and white photos blown up to poster size showing that dreadful day. I quickly passed by the ghastly images of people walking with bloody wounds, their skin dripping like wax from a candle. Trying to divert Laughlin's attention away from the images, I explained to him during times of war, service members aren't the only causalities— children and parents suffer too.

The museum poignantly depicted how atomic bombs don't discriminate between the young and old, soldiers and civilians. Since the bomb fell during the day, children attending school died, and others suffered unimaginable burns from the radiation.

Behind a glass casing, a tricycle, owned by a three-year-old exposed to the radiation, sat twisted like it was made of clay. A pocket watch belonging to a man riding his bicycle had stopped at the exact time the bomb dropped. We read a young girl's story of how she'd made a thousand paper cranes in the hospital after being diagnosed with cancer from the atomic bomb radiation.

Touring the museum, the memorials of death and destruction were heartbreaking. I thought about our Japanese neighbors—how humble and respectful they were to us. Would I have treated them as kindly if they had dropped a bomb on my neighborhood?

As we walked through the museum, I glanced at the Japanese people. Some studied the photos intently. Others wiped their eyes. They were curious like me, wanting to learn, to understand why any country would drop a bomb which killed thousands of innocent people. How are they so kind and forgiving to the Americans who lived among them?

Overwhelmed by the deaths, the destruction, the pain inflicted on many lives, and the incredible power of forgiveness—I let my tears fall.

At one exhibit, Laughlin stood studying a gigantic globe, dotted with red flags over the continents like seeds in a watermelon. He wanted to know what the red flags stood for. I read the letter on display from the Mayor of Hiroshima.

The flags represented countries in the world with the capability to launch nuclear weapons. Trembling at the thought of a nuclear world war, I didn't share this information with Laughlin. Instead, I said the flags represented countries needing to work on world peace.

As we left the tour, we saw a huge, thick, hardcover book lay open on a table. Next to it, a notice said, if we wanted to promote world peace and prevent future incidents like Hiroshima and Nagasaki from happening again, to please sign the book. That day, we left two signatures from a small town in Georgia.

When we met up with Mark and Ryyan in the lobby, thier pink eyes and glum faces reflected their emotional journey. Our guide announced we'd meet at the pier and take a ferry to Miyajima Island.

Riding across the Seto Inland Sea, cool water sprayed on our faces from the boat's motor, helping lighten our mood from the museum. As we approached the island, a huge torii gate floated on the water like a buoy.

Exiting the boat onto a street teeming with tourists, Laughlin shouted, "Look at all the deer, Mom."

They were everywhere. Not like the ones in our backyard in Georgia, leaping about in a frantic attempt to get away from humans. But crowds of deer, their hooves clicking on the pavement, nibbling from the trees, and scrounging for scraps on the sidewalk.

"The wild deer are from the island's forest. During the day, they wander among the people and retreat to the forest in the evening," said our guide.

Signs were posted everywhere not to feed them. We soon learned why, when a tourist petted a gentle-looking deer and handed him a treat from his pocket. The deer nudged him for another treat, and the man refused. Standing on its hind legs, the deer boxed the man with its front hooves.

A group of onlookers surrounded the man and shooed the deer away. We drifted away bewildered by the incident, clutching our snack bags.

Our guide said the island was small enough for us to sightsee on our own. She recommended we take a trek up the mountain to view the enchanted forest.

After a lunch of fresh seafood cooked in a blend of Asian spices and the sweet aroma of maple from momiji manjū, a local confection, we ambled onto a wide, paved road up the mountain.

Laughlin and Ryyan chased one another, while Mark and I strolled along the winding road through the forest. As we crossed bridges over clear streams, Mark slipped his hand in mine, while the sun revealed brilliant colors throughout the lush forest, and the fragrances of wild flowers clung to the mountain air. I closed my eyes and thanked God for the moment.

Without enough time to reach the top, we plodded back down, savoring the last moments of peace. We returned to the dock—still swarming with deer and people—and cruised back to Hiroshima, where our tour guide gave us time to freshen up and rest before dinner.

We were in for a workout when our guide said we could walk the fifteen-minutes to the restaurant from the hotel. Her short, quick steps had us jogging. Noticing our struggle to keep up, she slowed her pace allowing us to peruse the downtown window displays and sidewalk cafés.

We followed her into an alley and entered a building's side door. We trailed her up a narrow staircase where curry and ginger spices floated on the air. We squeezed behind her at a door on the second floor landing, as our guide knocked on the door. An attendant opened the door, and oriental music from the Koto rose over clanking dishes and the chatter of conversations. The attendant sat us at a large grill where guests waited.

The chef handed us a menu in Japanese and English. While we studied the menu, he entertained the children making animal figures and a flaming volcano from chopped cabbages.

After he took our orders, we gazed in amazement while our chef cooked fifteen meals for five families and served them all at once, steaming hot and delicious.

Since no great meal could be complete without dessert, I opted for the green tea ice cream. Ryyan chose strawberry and Laughlin chocolate. When Mark requested butter pecan, I gave him a you've-got-to-be-kidding look. The chef returned with large bowls, heaping with ice cream, with every request granted.

For the rest of the tour, we were free to explore the city on our own. Using our maps of the city, we took our time and studied the sites of Hiroshima.

Our last night, we left the boys in their hotel room and took a walk along the pier. Waves from the sea splashed softly against the dock, city lights in the distance illuminated the sky. A couple, both with grey hair, strolled past us holding each other close, speaking softly and sneaking kisses.

"You think we will grow old together?" I said.

"Let's try," Mark said, wrapping his arms around me.

The morning of our departure, Mark took our suitcases down to load onto the bus while I checked on the boys. In their room, Laughlin dressed to go, sat on the bed, watching television.

"Ready," I said.

"No, Mom. Let's stay. This place is nice."

"And the price is nice, too," I said. "Where's Ryyan?"

"In the shower."

"Okay, grab your suitcase and wait downstairs."

I knocked on the bathroom door and told Ryyan to hurry, grabbing a suitcase sitting next to the door. Back downstairs, I waited with Mark, Laughlin, and the other passengers near the elevator.

Minutes later, the elevator door opened, revealing Ryyan in a fluffy white robe, his arms stuck out from the short sleeves, and the bottom of the robe hanging above his knees. A pair of slippers covered half his feet. Mark and Laughlin roared with laughter—I held mine in.

"You took my suitcase, Mom."

Chagrined, I looked down at the luggage on the floor next to me. On the bus ride home, we didn't get much rest. We were too busy ribbing Ryyan about his designer robe and slippers.

CHAPTER 21—MARRIAGE AND MISSIONARIES

Yolanda volunteered to keep Laughlin while we attended the marriage retreat. She also updated our train map to Tokyo, since the odds of another angel waiting to rescue me were slim. Joe's parents invited Ryyan to stay the weekend. With my luggage packed, I peeked into Ryyan's room. He sat on the side of the bed, shoulders drooping.

"What's wrong? Why aren't you ready?" I asked. His overnight bag lay sprawled on the floor.

"Why didn't you tell me we were staying another year?" he said. "Yesterday, one of the kids at school overheard his parents talking about the teachers who signed contracts to stay. They mentioned you and Dad."

I couldn't dismiss Ryyan's anger. In my desperation to convince Mark to stay, I had failed to ask Ryyan how he felt about another year.

"I'm sorry. We didn't have much time to decide."

"You always get your way," he said. "I left my home and friends too. You told me we'd be home my senior year."

"We will."

"You'll find a way to trick Dad into staying," he said, kicking his book bag.

"What's going on?" Mark said, entering the room.

"Ryyan found out last night from friends we're staying another year," I said.

"Wait for us in the car," he said to me.

I left the room, brokenhearted for Ryyan and jealous of Mark. Whenever the boys and I quarreled, Mark refereed. Always the good guy, level-headed and compassionate.

Mark got into the car.

"Is he coming?" I said.

"Yeah. We had two weeks to think about returning. He's only had a night."

We climbed the steep steps exiting the Shinjuku train station and merged onto a sidewalk with pedestrians hurrying toward downtown Tokyo. The crowd pushed us in the right direction toward the New Sanno. We entered the bustling hotel courtyard where other couples were unloading their luggage. Mark and I checked in, received our welcome packet, dropped off our luggage, and joined the other couples in the dining room for lunch.

Christy, a friend from church, waved us over to her table. She introduced her husband, James. When Mark learned he had a Harley, they bonded as only men can do over an expensive machine built for speed.

After lunch, we gathered in a large conference room. Our presenters introduced themselves as a husband-and-wife team. Tim and Amy were missionaries in Japan and wanted to share their marriage journey with us.

Tim said he and Amy had married not understanding God's design for marriage. Tim, newly married, rode the waves of courtship—enthusiastic about his role as a new husband. They settled into the realities of work, managing a household, and children. What they didn't anticipate was their worldly view of marriage, their own selfishness, and the trials of life would burden their marriage. Which led to fighting, a quiet storm, isolation.

Amy said Tim had adored her during their courtship. Yet, a year after the wedding, Tim went from being a loving, attentive husband to one who spent most of his time either at work or with his hobbies. The oneness Amy had had with Tim vanished. When she approached him to talk about it, he never wanted to and blamed her for not being satisfied. Amy became controlling and manipulative, which pushed Tim further away. But through Christian counseling and a seminar like this one, Tim and Amy had come to understand God's design for marriage.

Tim explained God wants us to have a oneness with our spouse and to mirror his love for us within our marriages. If, as husband and wife, we fail to put Christ first, everything we seek within our marriages will fall short. Husbands and wives—two imperfect people—are joined together to serve God first and to serve one another. He admitted God had not come first in their marriage, and he alone provided for his family. Amy, a child when her parents divorced, wanted Tim to meet all her needs. Now, she understood how unfair it had been to expect Tim to do what only God can do.

Tim told us our marriages should reflect God's image on Earth. Satan, the enemy of God, wants us to think our spouse is our adversary, but we needed to remember our spouse is not the enemy. Satan wants to destroy us and our precious children who need their dad and mom.

After Tim prayed for us, he gave us workbooks with pages assigned to help us reflect on our marriages. We were to work in our rooms, where we wouldn't be distracted, and return in a hour to the conference.

Mark sat at the desk, and I sat on the bed. I flipped through the workbook, not sure I wanted to answer questions about our marriage, afraid they would stir up old wounds. I glanced at Mark—his head down, writing quickly in his workbook. I looked at the clock—we had plenty of time. Question one read list threats to your marriage. With one hand across my forehead, I picked up my pencil.

"Are you ready to talk?" Mark said, leaning back in his chair.

I took a deep breath. "Yes," I said.

"I felt threatened in our marriage when you went into the military. You had control over our money, how we traveled, and where we lived. Growing up, my dad took responsibility for the finances and the farm, my mom took care of us and the house," Mark said.

"I didn't know you felt that way. You didn't complain."

"Why complain? You had a commitment to the military, and I wanted to support you. Sometimes when you came home, you ordered me around like you were still on the job.

"Let's talk about our lovemaking," he said. "I know we've both argued a lot, but we shouldn't use sex to hurt each other."

That would mean forgiving the painful words Mark had said to me over the years. "I'll try," I whispered.

"Your turn," Mark said.

"Financial burdens caused a threat to our marriage. When you quit your job and went back to college, it placed a financial burden on the family. I had to pay the bills while you went to school. You never volunteered to help me. You counted on the money being there."

My tears flowed.

"And moving to your hometown, where I didn't know anyone, and you have friends from kindergarten. You told me we'd still travel when I left the army. The only place we traveled was to Mom's house."

I wiped my eyes waiting for the denial, blaming, and anger.

"I didn't know you were struggling. You did a good job handling the money. I would have helped if you asked me."

Mark sat next to me on the bed, and we put the workbooks aside. We talked about our surprise pregnancy with Laughlin, who we both agreed God sent to help us stay married. Added to a new baby, we were raising a middle schooler and teenager. Both Mark and I admitted we'd stopped making time for each other. We talked for the first time in years without getting angry or walking away.

When we returned to the seminar, Tim said we should gradually integrate what we'd learned into our marriages. We'd feel uncomfortable at first, trying to live God's vision of marriage. But we needed to remember, it took years to build the high walls around ourselves to avoid pain and rejection from our spouses. We have to fight with prayer to break down those barriers and to remember our spouses are not the enemy.

For the next session, the wives followed Amy into another room. She said Tim was in the conference room, speaking to our husbands from the book of Ephesians about treatment of their wives. She would share with us from the same book about how we are to treat our husbands.

Amy said we are to respect our husbands, even if they make a decision we believe is unwise. When their insensitivity to our needs hurts us, we needed to have forgiving hearts, like Jesus has for us when we disappoint him. Lastly, we must let go of hurtful memories, which only push us farther apart from each other.

Trust God with our husbands, Amy said, and pray for them every day—not praying they'll do what we want them to do, but what God expects of them as husbands and fathers. Living with our husbands, we find dwelling on their faults easy, but if we look closely, we can always find the good.

When the session ended, Amy surprised us with a choice of a gift card to the massage parlor, nail salon, or spa in the hotel. She advised us to take advantage of the time, because our husbands had something special for us this evening. Thankful for my gift card, I searched for the nail salon. I hadn't pampered myself in a long time.

A few hours later, I caught up with Mark in the lobby. He stood next to the fireplace, talking to James. Glimpsing me, he shook James's hand and walked toward me.

"Hey, you girls sure took your time."

"We had a lot to talk about and a gift card to use. You and James were having a good conversation."

"We agreed to ride our Harleys together when we get back to the US. How'd you like to spend the evening in Tokyo with me?" he said grinning.

"We can't afford that."

"Now we can." Mark produced a gift card of his own. "Tim gave all the guys one and told us to take you ladies out for the evening."

After a quick shower, I changed into a sundress and gold sandals to show off my new pedicure. With a light touch of makeup and curls in my hair, I danced around like a school girl on her first date.

Tourists and young locals, sporting spiked purple and green hair and tight leather clothes, packed the downtown streets of Tokyo. Lanes of cars, buses, and mopeds flowed into the city like an endless fleet of ships.

We maneuvered through a crowded sidewalk and darted down an alley, where we found a novelty shop. Inside, the scent of lavender and jasmine made it feel like summer. Mark browsed with me and even allowed the sales lady to try a fragrance on him. Smiling, he asked if she had the fragrance in motor oil.

In the Roppongi District, huge electronic billboards lit up tall brick buildings. They flashed advertisements and played music videos. Sitting near a large window at Jonathan's restaurant, we ate hamburgers and observed people flooding downtown Tokyo.

After dinner, at the Imperial Palace, we strolled under the cherry blossom trees—their pink and white blooms beginning to bud for spring. As the late evening crowds thinned, Mark wrapped his arm around my shoulder, and we strolled back to the hotel.

In our room, I called the boys while Mark took a shower. I hopped in next, lavishing in the hot water and green tea soap I'd picked up in the little shop downtown. Slipping into my nightgown, a warmth covered my heart, remembering our evening together.

Back in the bedroom, I expected to see Mark propped up watching TV, but the room was dark with only a sliver of moonlight streaming through the window. In the bed, Mark's body moved close to mine. I stiffened when his arms gently pulled me close. Squeezing my eyes, memories of hurtful words and disappointments surfaced. My mind went back to what Tim had said. Mark was not the enemy. I pushed back the old wounds and thought about how hard Mark was trying to make our marriage better. Jesus had forgiven me for the awful things I'd said to Mark. Now I had to forgive him. Mark's lips softly kissed my shoulder. I exhaled. Please, God, allow me to be Mark's wife. The passion I thought was lost in our marriage found us that night.

The next morning, Tim and Amy presented each couple with a certificate and prayed for our marriages and children. Through hugs and promises to keep in touch, we said our goodbyes.

Ryyan apologized for his behavior when we picked him up from Joe's house. He was proud of us both taking time to get closer without kids hanging around. Yolanda dropped Laughlin off, and before I could tell him how much I'd missed him, he wanted to know when we were leaving again. He had fun playing with Mickey, and Yolanda was a good cook.

The next day at school, Mark sent me a text message expressing how much he'd loved our time together in Tokyo. I didn't know how to respond. I remembered what Tim said—how over time, we take each other for granted, forgetting the words and feelings which brought us together in the first place. I had to give these new feelings a chance. I texted Mark back with Thank you, I did too.

Sunday morning, l followed the trail of sweet pancakes and bacon into the kitchen. Mark stood over the stove, and a platter of fluffy pancakes and bacon sat in front of the boys. Mark wore a nice shirt and pair of slacks, and the boys were ready for church.

"You'd better hurry up and eat, we'll be late for church," Mark announced.

"Church?"

"I told James I'd see him this morning."

I beamed. After a year and half in Japan, my husband was going to church.

Near the end of the school year, Ms. Phipps called Mark and me into her office. She thanked us both for staying on for a third year and said she'd made changes for the next term.

"Mrs. Smith, I want you to teach reading to students in kindergarten through third grade. Mr. Smith, I want you to teach first grade. Mr. Tony Robinson has taken a teaching position in Germany."

"Mr. Smith, I know teaching this age is new for you," Ms. Phipps said. "But I'm going to give you Mrs. Smith as an assistant for a couple of hours the first three weeks of school."

I waited for Mark to decline, but instead he said, "Sure, it'll be fun teaching first graders."

"How do you really feel about teaching first grade?" I asked Mark after we left Ms. Phipps's office.

"I'm okay with it. Plus, you'll be my assistant, and I can boss you around."

Doug, however, was disappointed. He'd just gotten used to his new team of Georgia teachers. "Breaking in new teachers and living in foreign countries is what DoDDS teachers do," he said.

We congratulated Tony on his transfer and gave him a going away gift. He'd been a great sponsor and friend. He told Mark he'd love teaching first grade, and gave him a box of books and supplies.

Yolanda spent the last week of school acquainting her Japanese students with Mark. Their long faces, while they sat around her kitchen table, were a strong indicator of how much they were going to miss her. Yolanda introduced Mark to everyone. Nervous, he told a joke to help everyone loosen up. Only bewildered soft brown eyes peered back at him.

Yolanda had already given Mark the lesson plans she used, and instructed him to assist her as she taught the lesson. Halfway through the lesson, Mark taught, and she assisted. After the lesson ended, parents and students came up to Mark, bowed and said, "Good Sensei."

Contracts were signed and goodbyes said to those who had transferred to other DoDDS schools or who were returning to the US. Although Yolanda was busy moving out of her apartment and packing up her classroom, we found time for lunch at our favorite Japanese restaurant.

This summer, we would visit David at Fort Bragg, North Carolina. He'd been assigned there from his unit in Germany. Laughlin was reluctant to leave Japan for the summer. He was older now and wanted to stay with his friends. I told him Gma would be disappointed if he didn't come home, and he wouldn't have to share a room with Ryyan for the summer.

That did it. Laughlin was ready to go.

CHAPTER 22—SUMMER OF FORGIVENESS

The Harley, tucked inside the garage, looked like a baby in a bassinet. After we'd agreed on the purchase, Mark found a dealership on Atsugi Base. Not a fancy dealership, but an old warehouse converted into a showroom packed with Harleys. The location didn't bother him. Mark found the Harley he wanted and had it delivered to our house in Georgia.

Mark had called Sam and asked him to store the Harley in the garage. Purchasing the motorcycle fit into our budget. We'd saved money living on Atsugi Base, and paid off bills. Mark signed up for a motorcycle defensive driving course, before he would get his license.

Laughlin begged Mark for a ride, but he refused even to test-drive the motorcycle on the backroads until he'd finished the course. Laughlin sat on the motorcycle seat and had fun riding in his imagination.

The morning after we arrived home, a concert of blue jays, sparrows, and whippoorwills woke me. Mark's side of the bed was empty, and his garden boots were missing. The cool morning breeze made me dress quickly in jeans, a sweatshirt, and sneakers. The aroma of brewed coffee met me halfway down the staircase on my way to the kitchen. I poured a cup. I moved outside into the dawn and sat on the porch swing.

A red sun rose behind tall, skinny pines, and a fawn nibbled on vines where the hay field and woods met. The boys were sleeping in their rooms and David was in Fort Bragg. Was this the peace we'd talked about in Sunday school? The peace God wanted me to feel all the time? Peace felt good.

We divided the summer between Mom's house and ours. On the farm, we fished and took hikes through the woods—something we had taken for granted before we went to Japan. We spoke with David often. I was elated every time I called and he said, "Hello, Mom." No more waiting on him to call, shouting soldiers in the background, or static on the line.

We planned a weekend trip to Fort Bragg, where David had made us reservations at the guest house. At the front gate, a huge sign read "Welcome to the 82nd Airborne Division."

The military police checked our identification as we entered the base. Soldiers marching in brown camouflage uniforms and helmets, with rucksacks and rifles slung across their shoulders, surfaced memoirs of my days leading troops as a 2nd Lieutenant.

David sat waiting on the steps in front of his barracks. He'd gained a few pounds and lost his desert tan since we'd last seen him. He jumped into the SUV, kissed me on the cheek, slapped his dad on the shoulder, and tussled with his brothers in the back seat. Mark and I started to fuss at the boys then laughed at each other. We were all together like old times, but soon we yelled for the boys to calm down before we had an accident.

Later in the evening, we went to a movie theater and a pizza restaurant. A year had passed since we'd been together, and everyone wanted to talk at the same time.

Back at the hotel, the boys played video games in their room. Mark and I relaxed in ours, reminiscing about the days each of our children were born—how tough parenting was, and the sacrifices we'd made in time and money for them, but how our boys were worth it.

The next morning, David took us to his room in the barracks. We entered the first floor of a three-story brick building with polished tile floors and freshly painted walls. A young soldier who looked Ryyan's age nodded his approval as we walked past with David.

On David's hall, we walked past doors painted in battleship gray, without names or fun decorations like college dorm room doors. Inside David's room were four twin-sized beds, all inspection ready, with military-green woolen blankets, white sheets pulled tightly at the corners, and pillows in snow-white pillowcases pressed flat against each bed. Invisible walls divided each soldier's space, with a locker and a trunk at the foot of each bed. Little had changed in the way a soldier lived since I was a lieutenant inspecting barracks.

David led us to his area in the far corner of the room.

"Here it is, my home away from home," he announced.

"Where's everyone?" I said.

"Most of the soldiers stay in town on Saturdays."

"I'm going to quit complaining about my space in Japan," Ryyan said.

David opened his footlocker, found a large, brown envelope, and poured out photographs onto the bed. We huddled around.

In one picture, David wore a camouflage helmet, bullet-proof vest, battle dress uniform all the color of desert sand, and was holding a large machine gun. "We kept these guns with us," he said.

Another picture showed David and several soldiers standing on a tank, holding their rifles in front of a tan-colored massive building with a gold dome. "One of Saddam Hussein's palaces," he said. David dug around in his footlocker, took out a card deck and spread them across the bed. "Here're Saddam's hit men. We were instructed to kill on sight."

David's voice faded, and I backed away from his bunk. Through photographs, war had become a reality, and David had quickly lost his teenage years to become a soldier.

Early the next morning, before Mark and the boys woke up, I got up and drove around the base. I found what I was looking for in an obscure corner of the base. The white clapboard building's steeple jutted into a clear blue sky. I checked the service times.

After breakfast, amidst grumbling that we were on vacation and shouldn't have to attend church, Mark and I loaded up the boys. Inside the church, a few people sat in the pews. The chaplain said because of the 82nd's frequent deployments to Iraq, most of his faithful members were away.

The message was inspiring, and the chaplain sang—standing in for his missing choir. The service was short. I was grateful—the boys were rolling their eyes at me.

After services, Mark reminded me we had a six-hour drive back home, and David had to work early the next morning.

Mark and the boys hung out in their room. I packed in the other room. A while later, the door opened. David and Mark stepped inside and closed the door behind them.

"Hey, what's up, guys?" I said, still packing our suitcases.

"Mom, I have something to tell you," David said.

"Why so serious?" I asked, closing a suitcase.

"I'm deploying to Iraq next month."

I flopped on the bed, looking at my twenty-year-old. "You just got back. How can you go again?"

"I've been here a year. There are soldiers already on their third deployment to Iraq.

How could I endure David in Iraq another year after seeing the pictures from his locker?

"Do your brothers know?"

"We know, Mom," Ryyan said, as he and Laughlin eased into the room.

Many arms suddenly surrounded me, squeezing me tightly. I heard Mark reciting the Lord's Prayer.

Back in Georgia, driving home from the grocery store, I tried to outrun the dark clouds chasing my car down the narrow country road. Thunder rumbled, and white flashes of lightening crisscrossed the midnight-colored sky.

I parked on the roadside. Sheets of rain poured from the sky, along with tears from my eyes. Tears for David—returning to Iraq and never having the opportunity to experience his young years—dating, college, first apartments. And tears for me, afraid if we left Japan and returned home for good, those threats to our marriage would return as well.

Please God, watch over my son. Put your guardian angels around him. Help me to trust you with my marriage. The rain stopped. A brilliant sun pushed through the clouds, leaving a glittering rainbow across the sky. Thank you, Lord.

Our last week in Georgia, I dropped the boys off with Mom, giving Mark and me a chance to be alone. Between traveling, work, and visitors since our arrival in Georgia, we hadn't spent time together. Amy spoke of how little quality time couples devote to their marriage. A friend recommended a bed and breakfast in a nearby town.

Giddy with excitement, I was like a bride planning for her honeymoon. I purchased cheese, grapes, fancy crackers, fresh cut flowers, and sweet tea at the grocery store.

Next, I shopped at the mall for much-needed lingerie. Victoria's Secret was a little too racy after wearing T-shirts to bed for years. I went to Belk's instead. The sales girl helped me pick out a short silk nightgown. Viewing myself from different angles in the dressing room mirror, with the weight I'd lost walking everywhere in Japan, and holding in my stomach, I thought I didn't look too bad for a mother of three.

Now came the hard part—getting into the house and packing without Mark asking questions. Next, I had to persuade him to drive the thirty miles to the bed and breakfast—not an easy feat, since Mark had become glued to the farm when we came home for the summer. I'd read about a wife who wrote a note to her husband inviting him to join her at a restaurant for dinner. I could do the same, only I chose a B&B.

When I arrived home, Mark's black Toyota truck was in the driveway. I entered through the garage and placed my note into one of the Harley's saddlebags. I entered the house through the garage. Mark sat at the computer with a frown on his face.

"I think we have a virus, and I need to clean the computer," he said.

My timing was perfect. Mark would focus on the computer, not on me, as I got down to business. I told him the drop-off had gone well, but I needed to go out again. I'd forgotten a few things.

"But you just got here."

"I know, but there's no food in the house."

"We can go out," Mark said. "The boys aren't here."

"No, that's okay," I said, and ran upstairs and grabbed my overnight bag, vases for the flowers, and the candles.

I left through the kitchen on my way out.

The screen door slammed.

"Hey! You gone?"

"No," I said. "Just getting something out the car."

I loaded up the car and ran back into the house.

"Are you going anywhere in the next thirty minutes?" I said.

"No, I need to get the computer straightened out, and this program takes some time to run," he said, studying the computer.

I kissed his cheek and crept out the door.

I opened the B&B room door to polished hardwood floors and a queen-sized bed in the middle of the room. The comforter, pillows, and drapes were hues of blue. The redwood night stands and table provided room for candles and flowers. A large picture window exposed pine trees surrounded by fluffy pink and white azalea blooms and a pond.

Falling back onto the bed, I allowed the plush comforter to embrace me, wanting to enjoy the room a few minutes by myself.

I checked the time. I had told Mark I'd be home in thirty minutes—forty-five had passed. I called. He answered the phone on the first ring.

"Hello, this is your wife," I said, trying to sound sexy over the phone.

"What's wrong? Why are you calling me? Where are you?"

"I'm fine," I assured him. "I want you to look inside the saddlebag of the Harley."

"What? What's wrong with your voice?"

"Nothing." I place my hand over my mouth to hold back my laughter.

"I read the note," he said. "I'm on my way."

I quickly made final preparations to the room and took a shower, inhaling the aroma of green tea soap.

Thirty minutes later, Mark knocked on the door. He grinned at me through his dark glasses, wearing his leather jacket, and motorcycle helmet under his arm. I pulled him into the room. His mouth fell open, looking around at the flowers, candles, and his wife wearing sexy lingerie.

"Here are the rules," I said. "No TV, no talking about the boys or school. Just us.

"Okay." He smiled, quickly taking off his riding gear, sliding onto the bed. "By the way, I love the new you," he said.

With scented candles burning, our favorite jazz music playing, and me wearing a baby-doll nightgown, Mark handled the rest.

Two days later, I found Mark in the garage with his helmet on and one in his hand. "Who's the extra helmet for?"

"You. We only have a couple more days before we leave. I want you to ride with me," he said, handing me a motorcycle helmet.

"Really? I haven't ridden a motorcycle in years," I said, inspecting the helmet, wondering how it would feel on my head.

"Let's give it a try," he said. "I've practiced riding all summer. We can ride down the road to the park. But first, there are a few things I want you to remember. Don't squeeze my waist, and lean into the turns with me. Got it?"

"Don't squeeze, lean," I said.

I slid my leg over the smooth, black leather seat. Mark started the Harley. My body vibrated with the engine's power.

I grabbed Mark around the waist.

"Don't squeeze," he yelled, over the Harley's motor rumbling throughout the garage.

I loosened my grip.

Mark balanced the Harley as we rode down the gravel driveway. He stopped the bike at the road, where sweet honeysuckle lingered near our mailbox. Slowly, he pulled out onto the highway.

On the Harley, cruising down the winding country road, leaning into the curves with Mark, I released David's deployment to Iraq and the upcoming school year. For now, Mark and I were closer and our children, happier.

CHAPTER 23—A PLEA FOR RYYAN

Our first morning back from summer break, I left Mark and the boys sleeping and walked to school. I wanted to get an early start preparing for the new school year. Mark needed help transitioning to the first-grade, and I had to plan for my new reading specialist position.

As I strolled along the sidewalk, our neighborhood was quiet with families in the US on summer vacation. From the Red Top, Fuji was concealed behind a wall of clouds, waiting to appear when the children returned to school. Mark's car raced up next to me when I walked home.

"Something's happened to David," I said, my body growing numb with fear.

"No, Ryyan," Mark said. "He's in trouble."

"Trouble?" Ryyan was asleep this morning when I'd left. What could have happened in an hour?

"The Navy's legal office called and said Ryyan was involved in a criminal offense with another teenager. They want us at the JAG office to see Lt. Murray. I left Laughlin at Andrew's house."

Ryyan? A criminal offense? I moved in slow motion getting into the car.

"Where's Ryyan?" I said, on our way to the legal office.

"He left the house for football practice this morning."

The secretary seated us outside Lt. Murray's door. Soon, a tall, slender young man with a crew cut, wearing a crisp, white Navy uniform, motioned us into his office.

"Mr. and Mrs. Smith, have a seat," he said, pointing to the leather chairs in front of a wide, mahogany desk.

"My name is Lt. Murray, and I'm the JAG Officer for Atsugi Base," he said, standing behind files stacked on his desk.

"A Navy Police investigation revealed that on the night of June 21, two teenagers—one of them your son—lit small fires on the nature trail, moved up into the housing area, and later, onto the school's playground," he said.

"Not Ryyan," I shot back.

"Let him finish," Mark said.

"Mrs. Smith, your son will have the opportunity to defend himself before a disciplinary board," he said through clenched teeth, obviously annoyed he had to deal with teenagers.

He walked abruptly from around the desk and opened the door with papers in his hand. My stomach tightened walking toward the door. "By the way," he said, "The board and I will decide whether Ryyan stays in Japan or returns to the US. I need to let you know we already sent the other teenager back to the US."

"Here's the report. The hearing is in three weeks at the Family Support Center. You can bring recommendation letters for the board members to review. The Navy CID will contact you soon." The lieutenant held his head high when we walked past. No "sorry this happened" or "I know your son wouldn't do such a terrible thing" or "we'll find out the truth." He just closed the door.

Back in the car, Mark and I skimmed over the report. I thought back to the day before we flew home to Georgia for summer break. We'd all gone to church and afterward to the cell phone store. Later, we'd had lunch at a Japanese restaurant.

Ryyan had called his supervisor that afternoon and told her he'd be late for work—that he needed to pack for summer break. I'd dropped him off at work. I needed my car to run errands.

After I picked him up from work, we drove home. He'd chatted past midnight with his friends over the computer until I'd made him go to bed. Why would Ryyan set fires on the base back in June when we were leaving for Georgia the next day? We wouldn't need a hearing if both Ryyan's supervisor and I vouched for where he was that night.

"Once the lieutenant hears Ryyan's side of the story, he'll have to apologize," I told Mark as we drove home. The phone rang as we entered the apartment.

"Mrs. Smith, this is Detective Johnson from the NCIS. I need to speak to your son about the incident in June."

"Ryyan's not here. He's at football practice," I said, turning on the speakerphone so Mark could hear.

"When he gets home, bring him to the police station for questioning."

"Today isn't a good day. We haven't even had a chance to speak with him yet. We just flew back from the US yesterday."

"Ma'am, we can pick him up," the detective said.

"Like a criminal?"

"This is a courtesy call. We don't have to wait for him."

Mark took the phone from me. "I'll have him there after football practice," he said.

Before I had time to react to the phone call, Ryyan walked through the front door with his football gear.

"Have a seat," Mark said. Ryyan sat on the edge of his chair. "Your mom and I have just returned from the Navy Legal Office. The attorney said you and another teenager set fires on base before we left for summer break."

"I was with him, but I didn't set any fires," Ryyan said, eyes darting back and forth between Mark and me.

"How?" I said "I took you to work and brought you home."

"When you dropped me off, I went to work, but my boss said she was closing early and didn't need me anymore. At the food court, I ran into one of my friends."

"What did you guys do at the food court?" I said.

"We left and went for a ride."

"Instead of coming home, you rode around the base with your friend?" I said.

"I didn't know what he was going to do," Ryyan said.

"The police have asked us to come down to the station," Mark said. "They have questions for you. Tell the truth. No matter how bad it sounds."

Ryyan took a shower, and they left for the police station.

I stood outside on our balcony, looking into the forest. With Ryyan at the scene where the fires were set, I would have a hard time proving his innocence to Lieutenant Murray.

I picked up Laughlin from Andrew's house while Mark and Ryyan were gone.

"Is Ryyan in trouble?" Laughlin said.

"Why?"

"Dad answered the phone and said, 'Ryyan.' He dropped me off at Andrew's house.

"I don't know yet. I hope not."

Two hours later, Mark walked into the apartment. Ryyan followed, his head bowed.

"Mom, I've got something to tell you." He walked over to me, tears in his eyes. "I set a fire. I put lighter fluid in the trash can on the Red Top and threw in a match. I'm sorry."

Sobbing, he buried his face into my shoulder, I embraced him, heartbroken and disappointed. What can I say? What would I want my mom to say to me? "I forgive you, Ryyan."

"May I go to my room?" he said, suddenly looking older than his sixteen years.

"Not yet," Mark said, his voice trembling. "There's something we need to do. Come here, Laughlin."

We formed a circle and held hands. Mark said the Lord's Prayer.

The hearing was in two weeks. I needed to inform Ms. Phipps. She had become close to the family, seeing us each Sunday at church. As a mother of two adult children, she was very understanding, saying the teenage years were difficult for young people trying to find their way.

She offered to help and said we were in her prayers. The excitement of starting our third year in Japan quickly waned. I couldn't help feeling guilty about Ryyan. If we'd gone home after two years like we'd originally planned, he might not have gotten into trouble.

Waiting on the hearing, Mark and I still had a responsibility to teach, even with the heavy burden we now carried. If the board recommended Ryyan return to the US, what were we going to do? We couldn't send him to stay with Mom and Pops.

We were having trouble keeping up with our teenager, how could two seventy-year-olds? And what about Ryyan? How would he feel if he was sent home without us?

A letter came from David. He had arrived in Iraq and was assigned to the 503rd Maintence Company. His job required he'd fly in a helicopter, criss-crossing the desert, fortifying Humvees. Their mission was critical. Too many soldiers were wounded or died from the deadly IEDs set by the Iraqi soldiers. He said viewing the smoldering wreckage of vehicles blown to pieces by the deadly explosives, and the death and injury they caused, would remain with him forever. God hurry up and end this war.

In a couple of days, school would start. I could focus on teaching in my classroom—not the hearing. Mark needed little help from me transitioning to the first grade. The first grade teachers were ready to help him adjust. They supplied materials for his bulletin boards and helped him make them appealing to first graders. The room was already decorated with a rocking chair and a red, orange, yellow, and green checkerboard carpet for the children to sit on during story hour. A volunteer mom also came to help, making nametags for each child's cubby and folder.

I assisted Mark with his students the first weeks of school. I tied shoelaces, wiped noses, and took students to the bathroom. His six-year-olds loved his Boy Wilson stories, and when the aircraft and ships went out to sea, they called Mark 'Daddy.' I missed our times together during lunch break and planning, but helping Mark and my new reading job took up any extra time.

Every evening for two weeks, Ryyan worked on his apology letter for the incident. Mark and I had him rewrite it several times, and listened while he practiced reading. I gathered recommendation letters from Ryyan's football coach, teachers, and his supervisor at the food court. I pulled out his academic and athletic awards and made copies for the board members.

Our first Sunday back to church, Mark and Ryyan stood in the aisle moving row to row passing the collection plate. They both had volunteered to become ushers before we left for the summer. Members had heard about the fires, but instead of shunning us or gossiping, they gave us encouragement, support, and prayer. Ryyan's youth pastor wrote a letter.

The night before the hearing, lying in bed, Mark pulled me close.

"We'll get through this together," he said.

The morning of the hearing, Mark and I left lesson plans for our substitutes, and Laughlin walked to school. Ryyan entered the family room with a fresh haircut, dressed in black slacks, a white shirt with a tie, and dress shoes.

He read his letter to us again, folded it and placed it inside his pants pocket. I put all the letters, awards, and certificates into a large envelope. We held hands, said our prayer, and went to the hearing.

We had no trouble finding the conference room on the first floor of the Sunday school building. Even though we were early, the lieutenant was already waiting at the door. Entering the room, I flinched when I saw the long table with four people seated behind it, all inspecting Ryyan as he entered the room.

The lieutenant took his seat in a high back chair between the other board members. He motioned for Ryyan to sit in a chair facing them. He introduced the lady to his left as the family housing director, and the man next to her as the investigator. To his right sat two men in Navy Police uniforms—the officers who'd gone to the scene that night.

The person the lieutenant described as he read the incident report sounded like a troubled teen who'd intentionally tried to set the base on fire. After he finished, he asked Ryyan for any recommendation letters. Ryyan handed over his packet. The lieutenant passed each board member a copy. They flipped through the pages.

"Do you have anything to say?" the lieutenant said.

"Yes, sir," Ryyan answered. He stood up straight, unfolded his letter, and began to read.

A cell phone rang. The lieutenant glanced down at his phone, stood up abruptly, and with the phone to his ear, walked quickly out the door. Ryyan continued to read while the board members listened. Wasn't the hearing going to stop until the lieutenant returned?

When Ryyan finished reading, the lieutenant came back in and took his seat. "The board will take into consideration all the evidence presented, and will notify Ms. Phipps of its decision," he said. "You're dismissed."

As we left the room, the lieutenant and board members stared at Ryyan as though he'd received a life sentence. I paused at the door, ready to say how unfair the hearing was, when Mark nudged me along.

"They're going to send me back to Georgia," Ryyan said, his eyes moist, outside the conference room.

"We don't know yet. I'm proud of you, Son," Mark said. "You told the truth. Let's go home."

While we waited, I tried to maintain our school and home routines. We continued to pray every morning, asking God to keep us together as a family. One night after bedtime, I peeked into Ryyan's bedroom. He was on his knees, praying. I sobbed inside. I wanted our life back, and my confident, carefree teenager back too.

A week after the hearing, Ms. Phipps entered my classroom after school. "You've heard," I said, quickly sitting down.

"No, but the lieutenant called me. He wanted to know if you have family in Georgia Ryyan could stay with. I told him I didn't know. I also told you and Mr. Smith would never send Ryyan home alone—if Ryyan had to leave, the whole family would go."

I stared at Ms. Phipps in disbelief. How could the lieutenant think we'd send Ryyan back home without us? When she left, I hurried to the lieutenant's office without telling Mark. Confronting the lieutenant was something I had to do.

"Hello, Mrs. Smith," Lt. Murray said. "Come in and have a seat." He motioned toward a leather chair and waited for me to sit. This time, he sat next to me. "What can I do for you?"

"I want to see the Atsugi Base Commander," I said, sitting up straight, fighting back tears. I refused to let him see me cry.

"Why? We've had the hearing."

"I want to tell him who Ryyan really is," I said. "How's he's not a troubled kid. He's smart, loves sports, attends church, and shares a room with his little brother. Ryyan's accepted responsibility for what happened. I want the base commander to know the decision he's about to make will affect Ryyan forever."

Lt. Murray leaned forward and looked at me, his eyes soft.

"You don't need to talk to the commander, Mrs. Smith. I'll speak to him for you."

"What?" I said.

"I can't promise you anything, but I'll tell him about Ryyan."

When Mark came home with Laughlin after ball practice, he gaped at me as I told him what had happened.

"Prayer," Mark said. "Prayer."

The next day at school, as I crossed the Red Top on my way to pick up my reading students, I saw Ms. Phipps talking to another teacher. When the teacher walked away, Ms. Phipps briskly walked toward me, waving a brown envelope. As she opened her mouth to speak, a jet boomed overhead. When the noise began to fade, she shouted, "He can stay. Ryyan can stay."

My marriage leaped to a whole new level after our crisis. As parents, Mark and I had grown closer, coming together and sharing the burden of allowing Ryyan to take responsibility for his unwise decision. We strengthened our relationship by leaning on each other—not blaming one another.

A super bonus was we'd established a habit of praying together as a family. Although Ryyan could stay in Japan, there were consequences. Mark and I both decided Ryyan had to give up his job and his driver's license. Ryyan said okay. He'd learned an important lesson and still had his family.

CHAPTER 24—SENSEI MARK

Mark's Japanese students' first lesson in our home helped get us back to normal. We both rushed home from school and tidied up the house. Mark prepared his lessons while I made snacks for the students, except the sweet tea, which Mark made.

Mr. Takeda, Mark's oldest student, had recently graduated from college and now worked for a technology company. His job required working with American businessmen and he wanted to learn conversational English. Mark usually took him on a walking tour of the base. They'd often end up at the food court or Mark's classroom.

When they returned after one lesson, Mr. Takeda inquired about the two huge trash bags on our deck, waiting for disposal at the base's community trash bin. He wanted to know why our trash wasn't recycled. Mark explained Americans were not thrifty like the Japanese. Recycling was a choice in America. Mr. Takeda said, "No choice in Japan. Big fine."

Sometimes Mr. Takeda suggested he and Mark leave the base and walk the streets of Atsugi City. Now, Mark became the student.

Mark's youngest students were a sister and brother—six-year-old Nanako and four-year-old Haru. Their mom and dad waited patiently on the couch while Mark gave the children a lesson. Mark used a reading program that allowed the children to see an object, along with the English name, and hear the object's name pronounced over the computer. Nanako eagerly and quickly repeated the names, her eyes fixed on the screen. She waited expectantly for the praise Mark gave her each time. Haru, on the other hand, squirmed in his seat and kept turning around looking at his parents. Halfway through the lesson, he'd jump out of his chair, and run sit on his dad's lap.

After the third lesson, only Nanako showed up with her mom. Haru was too young to learn English, his mom said. Mark agreed. Nanako's mom sat with her and learned English too. Once, after a lesson, she tried to pay extra, but Mark said no. He didn't charge for listening. After all, how was Nanako going to take lessons if her mother didn't bring her.

Yoshimi and Naomi were sisters who attended middle school. Their mother, Akemi, would sit quietly on the couch, smiling at Mark and the girls during their lessons. After the girls had attended a couple of lessons, I decided to try my beginner Japanese on Akemi. I introduced myself in Japanese, but she replied in English. She saw my surprise and said she'd learned English in school. Talking to me gave her a chance to practice.

Akemi and I soon had conversations about our families, jobs, and living in Georgia and Japan. During a lesson, she studied David's picture on the wall in his military uniform.

"First son, you miss very much," she said.

"Everyday," I said.

The girls were smart and quickly bonded with Mark, adapting easily to his technique of using arts and crafts projects to teach English. They giggled whenever Ryyan entered the room and, in their broken English, asked questions about him. Akemi said the girls took soccer, math, and piano classes in addition to English. I admired their commitment to the English class.

Akemi occasionally brought me a neatly wrapped package when she and the girls came for lessons—usually a hand towel, notepad, or food item. One visit, she unwrapped a miniature box. Inside were pieces of white, rubbery meat, shaped like a long arm with suckers attached. She grinned and held up the box—waiting for me to take a bite.

"What's this?" I said chewing what seemed like minutes on the rubbery meat.

"Octopus," she said, smiling.

I squeezed my throat and swallowed hard. Afterward, my food items came from the bakery.

One lesson, Naomi came to the lesson without Yoshimi.

"Where's Yoshimi?" Mark said.

"In the hospital. Her stomach hurts," Naomi said.

The lessons were quiet that day. Before they left, I asked Akemi if we could visit Yoshimi at the hospital.

"Yes," she said, her face brightened as she wrote down the hospital's address and directions.

After church on Sunday, we went to visit Yoshimi. A group already occupied the room when we entered. Akemi introduced her husband, mother, father, and sister.

Yoshimi lay in her bed, thin and pale. Lifting a weak arm, she motioned Mark to her bedside. He gently took her hand, telling her to get better and return soon to her lessons. She gave Mark a weak smile.

The compassion he showed Yoshimi touched a place for him in my heart I thought was gone forever. Was this what Amy meant, watching for the good in my husband? Mark gave Yoshimi a gift. The family bowed low as we left the room.

Yoshimi missed three more lessons, but returned—healthy, happy, and ready to learn.

Mark sometimes extended English lessons to outside the apartment for his students. We went bowling at Parcheesi's, to the food court, toured our school and classrooms, and played on the Red Top—while Mt. Fuji smiled down on us.

Once, I substituted for Mark. Akemi and I decided to take the girls and Laughlin to the Food Court and the Red Top. As Laughlin and the girls played, the clouds drifted away from Mt. Fuji. Akemi, gazing at the mountain, said her people had a custom to climb Mt. Fuji once in their lifetime. A temple stood at the summit where gods held answers to many prayers.

One Sunday, Akemi and the girls joined us at church. When Bearson spotted them, he quickly came over, introduced himself, and handed Akemi a chapel Bible translated into Japanese. Bearson beamed sharing his faith with Akemi.

With the first weeks of school over, Mark no longer needed my assistance with his first graders. He stayed after school late a few weeks, planning lessons, stuffing folders, and assessing his students' classwork. I asked him why he worked late. He said reading first-grade writing on corn bread paper was tough on the eyes.

When I peeked into his classroom, everyone was busy with their different activities. During story time, Mark sat in his rocking chair with his six-year-olds, cross-legged, and starry-eyed as he read. Ms. Phipps said Mark had adjusted well to first grade.

Teaching reading to first through third grade challenged my organizational skills and time management. I worked late several evenings scoring reading assessments and entering data onto the computer. I read and chose books for each grade level. After practicing sounds and sight words daily, my students were ready to read books independently. The reward came watching students go from struggling readers to proficient.

On Thanksgiving, Mark invited his Japanese students to the Thanksgiving dinner on base. Their eyes widened at the large gathering and the long tables covered with trays of food. We watched the football games and troops from Iraq saying hello to their families on the large TV screens. Once again, with David's absence, Thanksgiving dinner lost its taste.

The Food Court had a eight-foot Christmas tree and Santa, which was great place for Mark to have his last lesson for all his students before Christmas break. I brought along eggnog and homemade sugar cookies, and we ordered pizza. We were delighted when Bearson and the choir assembled around the Christmas tree and sang carols.

David called, thanking us for his gifts. We said a prayer over the phone asking God to bring us all together next Christmas.

In January, Mt. Fuji's snowcapped peak sent a chill over the Red Top, ushering children inside during recess. I pulled my hood tight, crossing the Red Top to pick up my reading students. I glanced up at Mt. Fuji—early spring had started melting the snowcap peak, leaving black trails down the mountain. In a couple of months, the next school year's contracts would come out.

My life and marriage were good here. Why did I have to return to Georgia? I searched the summit remembering Akemi's words. Would God give me an answer at the top?

CHAPTER 25—PARIS IN TOKYO

"Hurry, Mom. The bus is gonna leave," Ryyan shouted from the car, wearing a black tuxedo, crisp white shirt, bow tie, and a fresh haircut.

Spring had brought blooming cherry blossoms and the prom. After the hearing, Ryyan hadn't wanted to go anywhere. But with encouragement from his football coach and youth pastor, he'd asked a classmate to the prom.

I drove toward Zama High, where prom goers and chaperones could catch a bus to the New Sanno Hotel.

We pulled into an empty parking lot outside the high school football field.

"What time is it? Are we early?" I said.

"No, this is when we're supposed to meet," Ryyan said, scanning the parking lot. "I'll call one of my friends."

A few moments later, Ryyan hung up the phone. "I missed the bus. My friend said I could've ridden with him, but his parents' car was full. My date is never going to speak to me again. Let's go home," he said, looking at the corsage he'd purchased for her.

"Wait, why do we have to go home? Call him back and ask if we can follow them."

"Mom, you can't drive to Tokyo."

"Who says I can't? I'll keep my eyes on their US license plate."

I pushed the March's engine hard on the back roads, trying to keep up. Weaving in and out of traffic, I strained to keep my eyes on the car's license plate. The car flew through a yellow light. The red light stopped me. I lost sight of the car.

"What are you going to do now?" Ryyan said.

Squeezing the steering wheel, I drove on. At a gas station, a car quickly pulled out in front of us. Ryyan's friend waved from the back window. "Whew, that was close," Ryyan said,

Traffic thinned out after we exited onto the expressway. We coasted into Tokyo.

I drove through the security gate of the New Sanno and parked. Ryyan hopped out of the car and joined young ladies in evening gowns and young men in tuxedos entering the hotel.

Inside, a whiff of dads' colognes blended with flowery perfumes lingered in the air. Soft music played in the background. A replica of the Eiffel Tower, covered in hundreds of miniature blinking white lights, stood in the middle of the foyer. Chandeliers were dimmed, and fresh flowers stood in vases on every table. A large banner across the lobby area read, "Welcome to a Night in Paris."

Ryyan and I noticed his date at the same time. She stood next to the fireplace, wearing a sky-blue gown with spaghetti straps. A bow in back hugged her young, slender body. Gold-laced sandals with skinny heels peeked out from beneath her gown. Her hair, pulled up into a bun, made her look like a princess. She wore no make-up except for clear lip gloss, and her only jewelry was a string of tiny pearls. Her cheeks turned pink when she saw Ryyan.

"There she is, Mom," Ryyan rushed over, hugged his date, and slipped the corsage onto her wrist. She tiptoed to pin on Ryyan's ivory boutonniere.

With an announcement the prom was about to begin, couples and parents drifted into a ballroom where a smaller replica of the Eiffel Tower sat on a stage with the band. White lights sparkled on the ceiling like fireflies on a summer night. A long table, decorated with pink cherry blossom petals, held a buffet of finger foods and punch. Parents and guests mingled and took pictures of the young couples until the music started for the first dance. The chaperons gently ushered us into the lobby.

I called Mark to tell him what had happened. He said I should have called. I leaned against the wall talking to Mark, feeling a glow all over, remembering our stay at the New Sanno. Before we hung up, he told me to drive home safely.

I lounged in the lobby with waiting parents soaking in the warmth of the hotel's fireplace. We talked and laughed about our own prom days, while our children danced into the night.

Midnight, the ballroom doors swung open, and teenagers strolled out with their dates. I waited in the car line while last kisses and hugs were quickly stolen. Tomorrow, blue jeans, T-shirts, and sneakers would replace formal wear, but tonight would last forever in their memories. Once inside the car, Ryyan took off his bowtie and tuxedo coat and got comfortable in the passenger seat. After he navigated me to the expressway, he fell asleep. No problem. I had plenty of American car tags to follow home.

Sunday after church, Bearson reminded me of the origami lesson he'd promised to give my students.

"How about this Friday?" I said.

While my students were at lunch, I picked up Bearson at the base's front gate. He got into the car, carrying a leather satchel.

"Do you live far away?" I said, driving away from the gate.

"An hour by train in the next city with my daughter. Then, I walk fifteen minutes from Atsugi train station to chapel."

"Why do you travel so far every Sunday to attend church?" I said, remembering the many times I missed church, and it only took ten minutes driving to get there.

"Atsugi Base closest American church."

"You speak English well."

"Because I sing in choir and never miss church," he said with a chuckle.

"What made you want to become a Christian?"

"My wife. Lots of joy in her life. I want joy too. She's in heaven now." He recited the first Psalm.

Eyes stinging, I admired Bearson's faith—a man not raised in a Christian home, but committed to serving the Lord and memorizing Scriptures.

I had work to do.

In my classroom, I left Bearson arranging squares of colorful paper on the table, while I picked up my students.

When we returned, I introduced the children to Bearson. They gathered around him at the table like a grandpa they hadn't seen in a long time. A few students spoke excitedly to him in Japanese. In both Japanese and English, he taught them how to make hearts, cranes, and other objects.

When students finished their projects, Bearson presented me with a gift—a "how to" origami book, and a supply of decorative paper. The students and I also presented Bearson with a gift—a T-shirt with the Lanham mascot on the front. We all bowed low, then the students and I gave Bearson a big American hug.

CHAPTER 26—MT. FUJI ABOVE THE CLOUDS

"After looking at the mountain for two years, let's see what it looks like up close," I said to Mark, not mentioning I had second thoughts about returning to Georgia. "I'll go," he said, "but I'm not climbing, mountains are for viewing."

I asked Doug for directions.

"Why do you want to drive? You can use the tour agency on base. They'll take you there," he said.

"Guess what, guys, I've reserved seats for us Saturday morning on a tour bus to Mt. Fuji." I told the boys during dinner.

"The mountain at the school?" Laughlin said.

"Yes, but we don't start at the bottom. There's a tourist center halfway up. That's where we'll start the climb."

"Yippee!"

"Not so fast, Laughlin," I said. "The climb could be dangerous. We'll decide if you climb when we get there."

"Oh, Mom," Laughlin said.

"I'm in," Ryyan said. "Most of my classmates have already climbed."

"Great. You can carry our backpack," I said.

At four-thirty Saturday morning, I eased out of bed while Mark slept soundly. We had another hour before we'd catch the bus to Mt. Fuji. In the kitchen, I packed a to-go breakfast. Earlier, Ryyan and I had stuffed a backpack with a map of Fuji, water bottles, energy bars, a first aid kit, and my cell phone.

The floor slowly rose beneath me while I made sandwiches. The apartment walls swayed like Jello, shifting the picture frames. The floor stopped moving. I released my grip on the counter. An earthquake. What if an earthquake happened while we were on the mountain? I said a quick prayer and finished making breakfast.

Later, we joined sailors and civilians on the last tour bus of the climbing season. Across the aisle from me, sat a nurse from the medical clinic on base. She and another young lady were taking inventory of the supplies in their backpacks.

"You ladies are really prepared," I said, eyeing their equipment.

"This isn't my first climb," the nurse answered. "The first time, I ran out of food and water. My climbing partner and I had reached the eighth station and had to turn back. We barely reached the bus before the mountain became pitch dark. This time, I'm ready."

I don't have a next time. I have to make this climb today. The early morning caused a hush to settled over the bus.

We woke to the lively soprano voice of our Japanese tour guide welcoming us to Fuji-san. The bus motor groaned slipping into low gear, maneuvering up the winding road, straining under the weight of passengers. Mt. Fuji from the Red Top and the bus window were vastly different. Instead of rock, the bus climbed past tall timber and vegetation lining the paved road.

Our guide braced herself in the aisle, and shouted over the straining gears of the bus. "Fuji-san is a sacred mountain. The Japanese have considered the climb a religious practice for centuries. You will not start from the bottom of the mountain, but halfway up, at the fifth station, Kawaguchiko. The climb to the summit and down takes eight hours— ten hours for rookie climbers."

Next came a safety briefing. If you got stranded on the mountain, the attendants at each station could call a helicopter for help and provide first aid. Those who were not climbing could visit the tourist sites at the fifth station.

The bus's brakes hissed, pulling into a dirt parking lot halfway up Mt. Fuji.

Kawaguchiko, fifth station, a large area cleared of boulders and rocks, had become a tourist haven crammed with gift shops, restaurants, and vendors. Colorful tents pitched in the center gave the station an amusement park appearance, not the starting point for a grueling mountain climb.

We exited the bus with Laughlin scampering ahead. At seven in the morning, the climbing excitement was contagious. Hundreds of tourists stood in line, snapping photographs at the trail leading up the mountain.

"Time for us to leave, Laughlin," I said.

"Mom, please, can I go?" Laughlin said.

"You don't have on climbing shoes."

"Other people are wearing sneakers," he whined.

"He can go with me," Mark said. "I want to take pictures anyway, and we'll turn back at the 6th station."

My family joined hundreds of Japanese and foreigners ascending Mt. Fuji, clad in hiking boots and lugging heavy backpacks. We trekked up the wide trail of lava rocks, boots crunching on stone, worn smooth over the years from millions of climbers' footsteps. I kept a steady pace, inhaling fresh mountain air, climbing past hundred-year-old fir and cedar trees, their knobby branches bent weary with age. Wildlife lay hidden deep within the forest. I soaked in Fuji's picture-postcard scenery, perfect weather, and the warm rays of sunlight.

After two hours, the crowd thinned. Ryyan and Laughlin were in front of me, while Mark trailed behind taking pictures. Hiking on the trail upward felt like a stroll through a national park —not a rugged volcano. When I arrived at the sixth station, Ryyan and Laughlin were waiting, sitting next to a wooden hut. Mark soon joined us. Snacking on energy bars and drinking water from Ryyan's backpack, we talked about the easy climb so far.

"Time to go back," I said to Laughlin after the break.

"I can make it, Mom. See, I've climbed this far."

Looking upward, I surveyed the mountain. The forest and wide trail disappeared into a cloak of dense clouds hiding Fuji's peak.

"Please, Mom?"

"If your Dad agrees."

"Let's go," Mark said.

Our group trudged up the now rocky trail. Ryyan led the way, his long strides causing Laughlin to run to keep up. Mark again trailed, taking pictures. I checked my watch—we had three hours left to reach the summit.

Gradually, the trail narrowed and turned into a zigzagging stairway of dirt steps embedded into the side of the mountain.

At the top of the stairway, after an hour climbing steps under the sun's rays, I was exhausted, sore, and thirsty.

How much further to the seventh station—and where are the boys and Mark?

A steep, narrow pathway led further up the mountain. A few feet ahead of me, posted among the rocks, were signs printed in red letters: "Danger! Falling Rocks and Sudden Wind Gusts. Climb at Your Own Risk!"

Squinting against the sun, I spotted Laughlin alone scaling boulders. I yelled for him to stop climbing, but a wind gust carried my voice away. I scanned the dirt stairway for Mark. I couldn't wait for him. Laughlin was climbing further up the mountain.

I quickly climbed boulders up the steep trail. Dizzy from the altitude and painful leg cramps, I continued to shout Laughlin's name. When I caught up with him, he stopped and turned around. I reached out and grabbed him. We both clambered onto the next boulder where thick, gray clouds enveloped us.

"What's wrong Mom, you're squeezing me?"

"Where's Ryyan?" I said. Trying to catch my breath. Watching for anyone to emerge from the dense clouds below us.

"I don't know. He climbed too fast," Laughlin said. "I'm thirsty."

"Me too," I said. "Ryyan has the backpack with our supplies. If you'd stayed with Dad at the bus, we'd have plenty water and wouldn't be stuck on this mountain."

Enormous tears rolled down Laughlin's cheeks, leaving trails through the mountain's black ash on his cheeks. Holding him tight, I cried too, feeling like the worst mother in the world. He'd only wanted to climb with us. It wasn't his fault I didn't want to return to Georgia.

"I'm sorry, Laughlin," I said, wiping his tears and mine. "Let's climb to the next station. Maybe Ryyan's waiting for us there."

With Laughlin in the lead, we climbed through billowy clouds and heaved ourselves onto the 7th station—a wooden deck built onto the mountainside.

I quickly scanned the deck for Ryyan. He wasn't there, but at the far end of the deck smoke rose outside a hut. A Japanese man sat outside branding 7th Station in Kanji onto walking sticks. Inside the hut was a make-shift store. Energy bars, chocolate candy, water, and first aid items lined the thin shelves.

"There's water," Laughlin shouted, pointing at the plastic water bottles.

A $5 dollar tag hung from one bottle.

"Remember, Laughlin, we don't have any money."

While I was trying to say "No money" in my best Japanese to the store owner, Laughlin said, "Mom, there're the ladies from the bus."

Emerging through the clouds was our rescue team. We sat together on the deck above the clouds, drinking water and eating energy bars. The ladies said the climb had become too steep for Mark, and he turned back.

"How do we get down?" I said, peering over the platform at the jagged rocks below.

"You don't," they said. "The trail back down the mountain at this level is too dangerous. You have to climb to the eighth station. There's a smooth path down."

The ladies purchased supplies for us from the store and gave us a bag to carry them in before we departed the seventh station. Laughlin and I joined them, this time climbing slowly and safely through rough terrain, to the eighth station. There the ladies encouraged us to finish the accent to the summit. Looking at Laughlin, I thanked them and said we'd had enough climbing for the day.

With the setting sun splashing red, orange and pink hues over the mountain, we began our descent. Hugging Laughlin, sliding down the mountain, I didn't need to reach the summit anymore. God had given me an answer.

Mark jogged toward the sixth station hut as we approached. He grabbed us both up into his arms. "I'm glad to see you two," he said, panting. "Ryyan's on his way down. He waited for you at the summit. Two ladies from the bus told him what happened. We'd better get back. Without a spotlight, we'd have to sleep on this mountain."

Pink skies turned gray as we waited on the bus. Ryyan and a few other passengers—including the ladies who'd helped us—hadn't returned yet. I got off the bus, pacing, straining to see up the trail as dusk settled onto the mountain.

Slowly, figures with backpacks and walking sticks moved toward the bus, like fog rolling into shore from the sea.

Before I could scold Ryyan for leaving us, one of the men from the group stepped in front of him and said, "Now don't get upset. Ryyan told us he'd climbed ahead and left his brother and you stranded without food or water. I want you to know, without his help, we'd still be up there. You have a great kid."

Speechless and bursting with pride, I got on the bus.

CHAPTER 27—SAYONARA SENSEI

On our last Sunday at the Chapel of the Good Shepherd, I clung to every song the praise and worship team sang. Mark and Ryyan walked down the aisle collecting the offering for the last time. After service, the pastor called them to the front, and presented them with a gift for ushering. Laughlin and I joined them as the chaplain waved the congregation up front to wish us farewell. Through teary smiles and hugs, we said goodbye to our church family. Bearson, last in line, handed me two large cranes and three smaller cranes—one to represent each member of my family.

"Happiness five times," he said, bowing low.

"Sayonara, my good friend." I said, eyes moist, embracing him.

When I walked into the cul-de-sac, the blue dollhouse came into view and music floated from Mewa's piano. The song sounded familiar. Amazing Grace. How did she know that song? I knocked on the door. The music stopped. The door opened to Mewa's surprised face.

"I miss you," she said, grabbing both my hands.

"Sayonara," I said. "We're going home to Georgia. Thank you for your friendship and sharing your neighborhood with the noisy Americans." We both laughed through tears, bowing and hugging on the tiny stoop.

Mark selected the new first grade teacher, who was replacing him, as the new sensei for his Japanese students. He was married and had a new baby. Mark and I had learned teaching English lessons was more than an exchange of services, but families coming together, sharing our lives and cultures.

We all met in Mark's classroom for the trial lesson and introductions. Mark had given the new sensei the lesson plans and while Mark taught, the new sensei assisted. Halfway through the lesson, the new sensei taught while Mark assisted.

When the lesson ended, Akemi and the girls spoke briefly to each other. They turned to the new sensei, smiled, bowed and said, "Good sensei." They hugged Mark and presented him with gifts. He carefully opened each one, blinking back tears, and bowing low. We, too, had gifts for Akemi and the girls. I'd found jackets with popular American football teams' names on them, and our school's T-shirts with the Lanham Crusader mascot on front.

I presented Akemi with an American cookbook and a case of sweet tea. Our last lesson ended with hugs and teary goodbyes.

A few day later, Akemi called and said she was booking their flight to Georgia and when could she and the girls come next month. Puzzled by the request, Mark and I decided Akemi and the girls needed one more lesson.

At the Food Court, we showed pictures with Mark riding on the tractor through rows of corn, peas, and green beans. On the back porch, the boys sat shelling mounds of purple-hulled peas throwing the empty hulls at each other. Cows grazed in the hay fields near the pond.

After eating pizza and ice cream, and taking lots of funny pictures, we promised to call once we were settled back home in Georgia.

The day before our flight to Georgia, we moved back into the Navy Lodge after clearing out our apartment and selling the cars. We had said goodbye to Ms. Phipps, Doug, and our colleagues. We would not come back after summer break.

I rolled over to an empty side of the bed. This time I smiled, while water splashed in the bathroom, and Mark hummed. I squeezed his pillow inhaling a faint scent of aftershave. A warmth covered my heart. The heart I had allowed to grow bitter and cold was slowly coming back to life. We were learning not to expect the same excitement and passion marriage brought those first tender years, but to experience a richer, more intimate relationship with each other in our marriage because we both know what God expects of us as husband and wife.

David called from Iraq and said his unit would return to Fort Bragg in December. His time in the army would be over, and he was excited about starting college. I'd learned not to get my hopes up during a war, but to trust God with David's safety.

Ryyan and Laughlin were staying with friends, and Mark wanted me to ride the train with him to Tokyo. He'd seen a camera he wanted at an electronics shop while we were at the marriage conference.

"Sure," I said, surprised he wanted to spend his last day in a crowded city.

We walked past the guards, out of the front gate, toward the Atsugi City train station. Mark and I, no longer visitors, blended in with the pedestrians on the way to our destinations.

On the express train to Tokyo, I admired, for the last time, Japanese houses with bubble-top roofs standing side by side in their quaint neighborhoods. Well-kept flower gardens in containers sat in tiny nooks along the storefronts. Futons and laundry hung on apartment balconies like flags. Lines of traffic waited patiently as trains flew by.

Mark and I exited the Tokyo train station where hordes of people pushed us into the city. I soaked in scenes of people shopping in extravagant stores in downtown Tokyo, and cars, buses, and motorcycles waiting for trains to pass. In a couple of days, I'd be back on our farm. The Japanese people's customs and language, those who had been my neighbors and friends, would vanish from my sight. Never my heart.

We stopped at a high-rise brick building with an elevator on the outside.

"What are we doing here?" I said. "Do they sell cameras here?"

"Be patient," he said smiling, and pressed the button.

The elevator opened to a familiar wall with smiling ladies wearing pearls.

"Hello, Mr. Smith. Welcome back," the Pearl Lady said.

"Welcome back?" I said.

"I have your package ready," she said, walking through the black silk curtain.

"What? How?" My heart thumped wildly.

"You don't have to know everything," Mark said.

The Pearl Lady returned and opened a white jewelry case.

"The DoDDs necklace," I gasped, throwing up my hands. "We can't afford this."

"You can't, but I can," Mark said.

Taking the necklace from its case, he placed the pearls around my neck. "I saved the money I earned from teaching the Japanese students," he said, grinning and revealing the dimples I fell in love with years ago.

The Pearl Lady handed me a mirror. The necklace fit perfectly.

"How did you know?"

"You told me about the Pearl Lady after the teachers' workshop two years ago." Mark explained. "I asked Joe at the marriage retreat if he knew how to get here. The Pearl Lady remembered you."

I touched the smooth pearls and embraced Mark. "I love you."

"I love you too," he said.

Once again, God had affirmed going home was the right thing to do.

EPILOGUE

Throughout the flight from Tokyo to Atlanta, knots formed in my stomach while I still wondered whether I'd made the right decision. If not, it was too late. We had shipped our household goods back to Georgia, turned in our resignation letters, and accepted teaching positions in Washington County, a small town thirty minutes from our farm.

The first day of school, Ryyan, now a senior, dressed in his military cadet uniform, prepared to leave the house. He would travel in the early morning darkness, driving on a deer-infested highway with limited on the road driving experience, for his thirty-minute commute to school. After he threw his football gear on the backseat, the family prayed. With watery eyes, I kissed him goodbye, asking God to watch over him.

Laughlin hopped into the car with us. We dropped him off at the elementary school up the road from the middle school where we would teach. Although starting fourth grade, he looked lost waving to us from the school's front door.

Mark was back in his comfort zone teaching seventh-grade middle-schoolers. I taught sixth graders for the first time on the next hall. How bad could teaching sixth graders be? They'd just left elementary school. After school, Mark asked me about my day. I burst into tears.

Our first Sunday attending church, we pulled into an empty parking lot. Mark called a deacon who informed us there were no church services on fifth Sundays. Instead of going home, Mark suggested we clean up the church yard. As we picked up sticks, I blinked back tears, missing Bearson and the Chapel of the Good Shepherd. Mark later spoke with the deacons and told them how disappointed we were. They agreed to open the church on fifth Sundays only if we taught Sunday school.

We soon settled into a routine of teaching, supporting Ryyan in his senior year, and helping Laughlin adjust to a new school.

David and a C-130 packed with men and equipment, arrived at Fort Bragg from Iraq at dawn. Walking down the ramp, the soldiers spilled onto the tarmac[1], wading into hugs, kisses and tears from family and friends. A month after leaving the military, David enrolled at Georgia College and State University majoring in accounting.

At the end of a stressful year teaching middle schoolers, Mark and I decided I needed to take a year off from teaching. Although we would miss my salary, we had saved money living in Japan and learned to trust God with our finances. While at home, I gathered my journals from Japan, and read and studied all I could about writing. Searching the internet, I read an article soliciting entries for the Guideposts Writers Contest. I won the contest after submitting a piece from one of my journal entries. Winning inspired me to write a larger piece about my journey to Japan.

During the end of Ryyan's senior year, he and I visited several colleges. After high school graduation, he made a surprise announcement. He was joining the military.

"How could you join the military after we just prayed your brother out of a war zone?" I said.

"I'm doing it my way," he said.

David took his brother to the recruiting office. Ryyan's first duty assignment was in Korea, next New Mexico, and then combat in Iraq.

Laughlin completed the fifth grade and after my year's sabbatical, I accepted a teaching position in Baldwin County, thirty minutes from our home, where Laughlin would attend Georgia Military Preparatory School. The third Smith brother to become a GMC Bulldog. Laughlin, active in his middle and high school years, participated in the marching band, won awards on the golf team, and played baseball

1

and football, all while maintaining the honor roll.

During the summers, Mark grew large, beautiful gardens. I'd get up before daybreak to help pick peas, shell them, and put some away for the winter. Seeing Mark's smiling face as I worked along side him, and receiving sweaty hugs and kisses was worth the work. Late evenings when gardening was finished, Mark, an English teacher, helped edit my work. In Tokyo, at the marriage retreat, we learned to appreciate each other's passions and help each other grow.

Mark and I began to supply our elderly church members` with fresh vegetables. We soon extended our deliveries to the elderly and sick in the community. We both found a new closeness toward each other and God—teaching Sunday school, delivering food to the sick and elderly, and spending quality time together.

After graduating with a master's degree in accountancy from Georgia College and State University, David went to work for a mid-level accounting firm in Atlanta. After several years, he decided to leave Atlanta and accepted an accounting position at one of the big four accounting firms in New York.

Ryyan left the military and pursued a degree as a software engineer at Georgia Tech in Atlanta. While in college, he found a church with an outreach ministry working with underprivileged children and the unchurched. Ryyan's senior year in college, he met his soon-to-be wife, Avery. He now works as a software engineer and is a Bible study leader at his church.

After graduating from high school, Laughlin took a different path than his brothers. He went from high school to college using the Georgia Hope scholarship. Laughlin graduated from the University of Georgia in 2020 with a degree in finance from the Terry School of Business. He's now employed as a financier working in Atlanta.

Mark and I continue to work hard at not allowing threats to our marriage to take our focus off each other as we age together and situations change. Now, empty nesters and retired school teachers, Mark has increased the gardens to grow more vegetables, and I write full time. By praying and reading devotions together, we can cherish each other through the seasons of marriage.

Looking back over the years, divorce would have stolen these wonderful celebrations with our children.

52 Birthday Parties

6 Junior/Senior Proms

3 High School Graduations

4 College Graduations

2 Master's Degree Graduations

3 Homecoming Trips Back from Iraq

2 Retirement Celebrations

1 Engagement Party

1 Wedding

Battalion Balls

Numerous Athletic Events and Band Performances

Numerous Awards and Honor Programs

Countless Sundays Serving the Lord Together

Children are a heritage from the Lord, offspring a reward from him. Like arrows in the hands of a warrior are children born in one's youth. (Psalms 127:3-4 NIV)

ABOUT THE AUTHOR

Janet Paige Smith is a 2012 Guideposts Writers Workshop winner and has written articles about marriage and families for Guideposts Magazine, Angels on Earth Magazine, and an anthology, Thin Places. Janet received her bachelor degree in social work from the University of Georgia, a master's degree in education from Georgia Southern University and a specialist in education degree from Georgia College and State University.

Janet has taught in the public school system for over 25 years and three years with the Department of Defense School System in Japan. Prior to becoming a school teacher, she served twelve years as a military officer. Janet is an advocate for families and speaks at women's conferences on God's design for marriage and how divorce affects children in the classroom.

She is the mother of three young men, two who served in Iraq and mother-in-law to Avery Curtis Smith. Janet and her husband Mark, are new empty nesters and both retired from school teaching in 2020. They enjoying spending time with family and friends on their farm in Georgia, where they write, garden, and fish.

To connect with Janet, please, visit her website at JanetPaigeSmith.com

Made in the USA
Columbia, SC
21 July 2021